Praise for Fran Gabino's Writing

Wonderful! Fran writes with such verve and energy. The anecdotes leap off the page. She definitely has a way with words. Description is certainly one of her strong suits. The story itself is at once nostalgic and funny. As someone who grew up in an atmosphere of isolation, her ring of family members, warts and all, sound like heaven to me.

Her extended family, for better or worse, was part of her life. Tiny details like Grandma working with her gravy over the hot stove bring the story to life. I especially like the way Fran integrated dialogue and authentic ethnic overtones. Well done! This is powerful stuff!

> — **Karen Michaelson, MS,**
> **Bemidji State University, July, 1999**

I like Fran's style —a bit of tabloid, vivid images, a certain sweetness and common (in the best sense) humanity, characterizes her writing.

> — **Astrida Butners, PH.D. Sociology**
> **Columbia University, NYC April, 1999**

Absolutely gorgeous...full of details that I care about. The hardest thing in writing is making complete strangers give a damn about what you have to tell them, and Fran succeeds handily. Bravo!

> — **David W. Koon, MFA**
> **University of Iowa Writer's Workshop**
> **July, 1999**

Crocodile Tears

and

Lipstick

Smears

a Superior Chronicle

Savage PRESS

Box 115, Superior, WI 54880 (715) 394-9513

First Edition

© Copyright 1999 Frances Ethel Oliphant Gabino

Cover design ©1999 by Jillene Johnson

ISBN 1-886028-03-6

Library of Congress Catalog Card Number: 99-64916

ABOUT THE COVER: March 19, 1946 Fran's eleventh birthday.
Left to Right: Doris Selma Raulerson, Frances Ethel Oliphant, Donna Mae
Sands and Lois Lena Paul.

Published by:

Savage Press
P.O. Box 115
Superior, WI 54880

715-394-9513

e-mail: savpress@spacestar.com

Visit us at: www.savpress.com

Printed in the USA

Crocodile Tears

and

Lipstick Smears

a Superior Chronicle

Fran Gabino

2-5-00

by Frances Ethel Oliphant Gabino

DEDICATION

This book is dedicated to my twin brother, the late Howard Damer Oliphant III and to my sister, Marie Damer Oliphant Marro, who share this chronicle.

Left: Frances Ethel Oliphant, age 7.
Center: Marie Damer Oliphant, age 9.
Right: Howard Damer Oliphant III (author's twin), age 7.

ACKNOWLEDGMENTS

Thanks to Mike Savage for his inspiration, kindness and friendship. Thanks as well to Liv Dahl, Sons of Norway, who edited my Norse spelling/syntax, and to Karen Michelson, Fergus Falls Community College, who edited the final draft. In addition, I thank my writing companions/teachers over the years, for their encouragement: Laurie Levy, Freelance writer, Chicago, IL; Tom Bracken and Allen Bates, Northeastern Illiniois University Chicago, IL; Anthony Bukoski, University of Wisconsin, Superior; David Koon, Laurie Klemme, and Jim McKean, University of Iowa Writer's Workshop. Special recognition is extended to my nephew, Mike Marro, who made this publication possible.

And finally, thanks to my long suffering friends/relatives, for sharing their insights, including Carol Gruber, Helen Heubsch, Barbara Turner, Larry and Le Ann Verkeyn, Sis Day, Cousin Rosemary Mockler Stone, Aunt Millie Oliphant Larson and Cousin Ruth Larson Wiberg.

I cannot and will not apologize for my life or my memories. It is my history, the things I felt, heard and saw. If it offends or does not match others' angles on the past, I can only advise that you write your own versions.

Memory is the diary

that we all carry around with us.

- Wilde -

The author, age 8, in her new hand tailored winter coat.
Grandma Larsen resized it from a hand-me-down adult coat.

Author's Notes

While rooting and tossing one day, I came across an article that inspired me to write my life story. The gist of the article titled *"How to Maintain Memory Fitness,"* is that the mind, like the body, needs constant exercise to stay healthy, especially as we grow older. One solution is to write your memoirs, a little at a time, beginning at the beginning. The result of this attention to long-past events supposedly will help you recall forgotten details and put things in perspective.

I like the idea of putting things in perspective, coming full circle - tying up loose ends. Since returning to Superior, Wisconsin, the place of my childhood/ young adulthood, after thirty-five years in Chicago, Illinois, I became overwhelmed by this completed-cycle phenomena. It was especially strong during a short stint I did as a Greeter at the local K-Mart. There I became reacquainted with people of my adolescence and was constantly reminded of past encounters. I often wondered, and sometimes asked, about their lives. The result was a sensation of completed stories, resolved mysteries. Thomas Wolfe wrote that you can't go home again, but I believe you can at least enjoy glimpses of what has been, could have been, even perhaps, what will be. The motto of my Oliphant, Scot's ancestry, is after all, *"What was, can be."*

Tuesday's Child Is Full of Grace

(...not to mention, full of herself!)

O n the night of Tuesday, March 19, 1935, long after the swallows had settled in at San Juan Capistrano Mission, California, befouling the paths of that popular tourist site with bird droppings, and the overflowing feast tables of St. Joseph's Day had been cleared, leaving celebrants slothfully lolling in gastric agony, my twin, Howard Damer Oliphant III, and I were extracted from our mother's womb.

Aunt Ethel Oliphant Wagner accomplished the deed in her front bedroom at 5922 Banks Avenue, in Superior, Wisconsin. Auntie's repetitious, lifelong opinion on the subject, "Giving birth is like having a huge bowel movement," was no doubt inflicted on our mother as she writhed and heaved, and finally, pushed her burden into the world.

Howard's breech delivery preceded the arrival of old Dr. Mason. For years after, Aunt Ethel recounted, "As soon as I saw those little brown walnuts, I knew it was a boy." She also noted that our mother still looked pregnant. When Dr. Mason finally arrived, he pronounced that there was indeed another baby. Aunt Ethel sprang into action and pulled me into the world at eleven p.m., ten minutes after my twin.

I wrote of the birthing in my 1987 application for "The University Without Walls" returning adult program at Northeastern Illinois University in Chicago, at age fifty-two. A capsuled biography was a prerequisite. Because I was seeking a BA in Communications/Creative Writing, I felt compelled to fictionalize the facts: *"I almost missed being delivered in 1935. Ten minutes after my brother was born, my midwife Aunt exclaimed, 'Good God, Marie, there's another one in there!' Forever after Auntie insisted, 'Frances came out feet first and has been sprinting ever since.' Too bad no one ever told me that you have to walk before you can run."*

I'm sure we squalling bundles of new life weren't much different from multitudes of other squalling bundles born on that same date all over planet earth. The luxury of sonograms, to take the surprise of gender let alone numbers from parents was not an option. Like unpredictable weather, what you saw was what you got, though at least with weather you could raise your wetted finger to determine which way the wind was blowing. In any case, everyone was ecstatic to learn we were twins, forever after fortifying in me the belief that we were special.

Aunt Ethel was justifiably proud whenever she related her achievement, especially since birthing was a relatively dangerous procedure when done at home. In spite of Dr. Mason's signature as attending physician, and the line for midwife being vacant on our birth certificates, everyone who ever repeated the story has confirmed that Aunt Ethel brought us twins into the world.

Once in a Social Ethics Topics class at NIU, my lesbian professor went off on a tangent about the overtaking of birthing by males, wresting that power from women, the latter's domain for centuries. That Janet Reno look-alike had an extremely low opinion of birthing in general. She stated, "Women are the ultimate baby machines." Her edicts on the subject were the only two of the professor's I was comfortable with, thanks I'm sure to the twin saga, imprinted on my brain.

Ma said, "I had a hard time of it. I was in bed for six months. Most of the time I cried, I was so ashamed to be pregnant again. Your grandma didn't much like Damer, especially since he couldn't find work." No doubt having sex in her parents' home with a man fourteen years her junior was a contributing factor to my mother's shame, imbued as she was from birth with Norse Lutheran morality mandates. That shame was only slightly tempered by her closeness to Grandma Larsen. Ma often said of her mother, "We were pals, more like sisters than mother and daughter."

Ma also said of her confinement, "I was afraid of getting

varicose veins." Her slender, well shaped legs were Ma's vanity. My sister and I inherited the Oliphant legs-gene. We both tend to put weight on easily and consequently are soft and round. Howard was always thin and lightly muscled. He got Ma's legs. Her pride showed whenever Ma said, "Howard took after my brother, Uncle Gunnar." She would have been devastated to have seen his swollen cancer-ravaged body as he lay on his death bed in December 1998. It was the only time I thought my twin resembled our Oliphant forebears.

Ma loved to relate that our entrance into the world was an event in South Superior, even though there was another set of fraternal twins there, the Dillons. In later years Ma regretted not taking our kindergarten teacher Miss Rockwell's advice, to keep a journal about us. Ma, the ultimate procrastinator, often said, "Don't worry; everything works out in the end," though nothing ever seemed to for her. She never got around to joining the Mothers of Multiples group in Superior, either.

My sister thinks Ma was too busy with the American Legion Auxiliary, Daughters of Norway and us kids. I think Ma didn't much like the members of that exalted group. She had suffered terrible humiliation and was ostracized by friends and neighbors in 1933 while pregnant with our sister, Day. After she appealed to the American Legion Auxiliary Welfare Chairman for help, Ma said, "The secret was out. Naturally when people heard an unmarried former President of the Auxiliary was pregnant, everyone knew it was me, because all the other ones were married." Mrs. Murphy, the Auxiliary chairman, assured her that secret arrangements could be made for Ma's marriage, but first she would have to get an appointment with the Relief Doctor. On her arrival at his office, Doctor Kyllo said, "I'm sorry but I've been informed by Mrs. Cadigan, the Welfare Caseworker, that we're not allowed to treat unmarried women." Grandma Larsen, incensed, shrieked, "Hyklere! Slike folk har vi ikke bruk for" (Hypocrites! We don't need those people!). She was no doubt reminded of her own ordeal when unmarried and one month pregnant with Uncle Gunnar. She and Grandpa were denied access to a Norse state church wedding. Records indicate that they, "..produced themselves before the Kristiania Magistrate on the eighteen of October, 1893 and <u>demanded</u> to be united, in accordance with the dissenter law of twenty-seven June, 1891, Section nine." In 1999 when I first gleaned that information, I knew in my bones that it was my grandmother who had made the demand.

Grandma Larsen urged Ma to go to "Gamle Mason" (Old Mason), their family doctor. In 1986 Ma recalled, "I was so ashamed. I cried and cried, when Ethel and I went to see him. He didn't even examine me. Dr. Mason was very old-fashioned. He believed childbirth was a natural process if you were in good physical shape." Doctor Mason told Ma not to worry, "Just let me know when you're ready and I'll come out."

In the end Ma caved to pressure from Aunt Ethel and my parents were married by Reverend Boe in the office of Concordia Lutheran Church on March 16, 1933, my father's birthday. In those days church law banned access to the altar in cases of adultery. Day was born six weeks later. As a teen my sister discovered *that terrible secret,* which increased her sense of being unwanted, unloved. My mother shared the whole story with me in 1954, during the early months of my own unwed pregnancy. It was her way of dissuading any marriage thoughts I might have had. She needn't have bothered.

At age ninety Ma told me she never wanted to marry our father. She said, "All I ever wanted was 'something of my own.'" I was fifty-one when I heard those words. The idea that my twin and I maybe weren't wanted, that we may still have been isolated particles floating in the cosmos, crossed my mind. I instantly rejected the thought. I now realize it was just too complex and agonizing for me to sustain at the time.

During that same 1986 interview when I suggested my twin gave Ma a lot of trouble in his youth, Ma snapped, "You were worse...running wild. I never knew where you were!" I still remember feeling as if I had been whacked with a two by four. Ma went on to blame a cohort for my downfall —the tall, dark, and scarlet-mouthed, Bernadine Kubarek. I spitefully mumbled, "I went haywire long before her," knowing full well my mother didn't hear me.

Ma wanted to honor Ethel by naming me after her, but Auntie protested, "No child should be cursed with that name," was her defense. They compromised by making it my middle name, Frances became my first, after Uncle Gunnar Stephan Larsen's wife. A smart move. The childless Larsens inundated us as infants with expensive gifts from Marshall Field's in Chicago, where during the 1930s, Uncle Gunnar was an accountant at the prestigious Medina Club.

I always wished I'd been named Helen, as the other twins I came to know at least shared their first-name initials. That was out of the question. Aunt Ethel never uttered her sister's name. Another sister, Aunt Rose, once told me, "Helen's the odd ball of the family." I didn't meet Aunt Helen until 1990, at my father's funeral. She was eighty-six then, tone deaf and hunched over her walker, her champagne-blond wig askew. During the inevitable visitation ritual discussion of how the deceased met his end —my father had collapsed on his kitchen floor from a heart attack upon return from grocery shopping— Aunt Helen's turtle-like head bobbed up out of her neck scarf as she shrieked from the funeral parlor sidelines, *"DID ANYONE CHECK TO SEE WHAT WAS IN THE GROCERY BAG!?"*

Like me, my siblings acquired family names: my sister was named for both our mother and father, my twin the third Howard Damer Oliphant in the clan, though our father was known at various stages of his life as Damer or Scottie. In his later years, after he'd become a trucker, my twin took on the appellation Crock, due to his admiration for Crocodile Dundee. My sister answered to three different names over her lifetime: Marie, her given name; Day, a nickname bestowed on her by Great-Grandma Waterston; and Maizie, her moniker amongst friends.

Once in a fit of sibling rancor, my twin and I taunted her by screaming, "Boulder Dam! Boulder Dam!" and tossing a lighted firecracker between her feet. In the end, it mattered little what we twins were called. Like most children, we answered to our nicknames, Sweetie and Peachy. Peachy called me "Numb." I suspect he was trying to say "Dumb."

The saga of our birth was engraved on the memory of an assortment of kinsmen, including Cousin Barbara Rose Wagner, who, though she inherited her father's reticent lassitude and slender round-shouldered frame, also acquired her Oliphant mother's snappish disposition. Until she descended on me twice in the 1990s, visiting for two weeks and then the second time, three weeks, Cousin Barbara was but a vague, lateral-offshoot on our family tree, as were all our cousins, due to the fact that even the youngest was nine years older than us.

While recounting family yarns, Cousin Barbara confirmed our mother's version of our birth —that my dad, Howard Damer Oliphant Jr.; my grandpa, Johan Michael Jorgen Larsen and her dad, Uncle Arthur Grover Wagner Sr.; were out in the wood shed chain-smoking, in nervous dread from each howl that echoed through the dark night. I could almost picture the scene — the just turned twenty-five-year-old father, wishing he was somewhere else, his elderly father-in-law, silently sucking on his pipe, eyes closed in contemplation of the sorrowful circumstances of life and father's withdrawn gnome-like brother-in-law, a World War I disabled veteran, who had been gassed on a battlefield in France, coughing uncontrollably with each drag on his Lucky Strike cigarette. Eleven-year-old Barbara kept skulking into the birthing room for a look-see, only to be shooed out by her strong-willed, take charge-mother, Aunt Ethel. "I just didn't see what all the fuss was about," Cousin Barbara recalled.

While narrating, "The night you twins were born," my cousin said, "I always considered you twins and Day my younger sisters and brother." Her statement nettled me, as I never recalled any such bond. Ma told me Barbara was a selfish, sly girl, based on an incident wherein Cousin Barbara, bolting a sackful of candy, refused to share any with my sister. Three-year-old Day sat wide-eyed and open-mouthed like a fledgling robin begging for angleworms. "I felt so sorry for Day," Ma said, a litany that dogged my sister's tracks the rest of her days.

Ma also said, "Barbara wasn't Aunt Ethel's favorite; she was her daddy's girl." I remember sensing something deceptive in her statement, in that Ma had once told me she was <u>her</u> dad's favorite, too, Uncle Gunnar, Grandma Larsen's. It occurred to me that that phenomenon of father/daughter, mother/son, was the norm. It could never be for me.

During 1990s visits to Aunt (Margaret) Rose Oliphant Mockler, who dropped her first name because grade-school classmates called her "Mugsy," discussions of Cousin Barbara's odd personality —her selfish abrasiveness and intolerance, sometimes arose. Aunt Rose said, "Barbara's not much liked by anyone. She's just like her mother, sarcastic, selfish and narrow-minded." Aunt Rose related how surprised she was one day years back when grade-schoolers Barbara and Buddy popped in for a visit. Barbara blurted, "Gee, you're fat!" Aunt Rose was nonplused. First, the Wagners and Mocklers never socialized as the sisters were sworn enemies and second, Aunt Ethel was much heavier than Rose. The girls' enmity dated back to their girlhood when as the two oldest, they vied for a power base to lord over their younger two sisters and three brothers.

Aunt Ethel's version of her and Rose's falling out claimed the incident was precipitated by a snide remark of Rose's but never revealed all the details. I have since learned from Aunt Millie that she and Rose were behind Ethel and their cousin Lucille Redman, pushing along in the throng exiting the Palace Theater on Tower Avenue, downtown Superior's main drag. The moment Ethel and Rose spied each other in the crowd, they launched a barrage of insults: "Piano legs!"... "Fat face!"..."Cow!"...Sow!" As the women's voices rose, people stood aside, first amused, then appalled and finally, excited at the prospect of seeing grown women doing battle. It was better than the Saturday night feature they'd just exited, and it was free, besides. The part in the mob widened to let the sisters through. Oblivious to the spectacle they had created, the sisters continued their verbal thrusts into the street, across Tower Avenue to the front of Woolworth's Five and Dime. The crowd trailing behind, suddenly halted en masse on hearing the shrieked utterance, **SLUT!** A gasp of disbelief shuddered through their ranks.

Rose, on hearing that final straw, struck the first blow. The melee' was on, resulting in Ethel's glasses getting crushed. A foot-patrolman had to separate the sisters.

I claimed ignorance when, during one of our chats, Aunt Rose asked if I had heard the story. Rose said, "I don't remember what the fight was about, but remember how ashamed I felt." I thought that odd, as Aunt Rose never failed to remember her first beau Kenneth Counter's birthday. He was killed in France during World War I and left her his insurance. Rose even remembered she had bought a brown velvet dress and chipped in twenty-five dollars with her dad, for a Victrola.

Aunt Rose did remember that on the disorderly-conduct court date she left home in her house dress, not telling Uncle Tom where she was going, in order to avert suspicion. Rose still remembered the judge's disgust with her and Ethel. Aunt Millie says she was appalled at both siblings and had no idea their enmity ran so deep, adding, "Til the day I die, I will never forget how embarrassed I was about those two."

Ethel and Rose never spoke again until when, at age sixty-one, Ethel lay on her death bed. Rose visited and was forgiven. I don't believe Ethel ever forgave their father, or Rose their mother, after their parents divorced. Well into her nineties, any hint of criticism of her father, brought Rose's shriek, "Don't you even THINK of saying anything nasty about my dad!" Helen once said, "My dad was a prince," while Aunt Ethel claimed, "Our father was a two-faced, skirt-chaser." Needless to say, it was the key factor that split the family asunder. The seven grown Oliphant children railed at each other the rest of their days, especially Aunts Ethel, Rose and Helen. My father and Uncle Robert clung closest to their mother, Aunt Ethel, and their youngest sister, Aunt Millie, because those women always took them in when things got tough. Uncle Fred and Aunt Rose remained close. Upbeat Aunt Millie, a devilish, high-spirited girl, became the family peacemaker as an adult. To me Millie was as youthful as her two daughters and like her brothers, loved the outdoors, hunting and fishing with them every season for years on end. In a fit of malice Rose once said, "Millie kowtowed to all of us; she wanted to be liked by everyone." Though surprised by her outburst, Aunt Rose's words produced an affinity in me for Aunt Millie, as it was a trait shared by my siblings and me, whose story I continue.

Day, who seldom spoke of the twin saga, says she only remembers what she was told. My sister has since begrudgingly admitted how excited she was to see two babies on the morning after, when Grandpa Larsen took her in to see us. Ma said that twenty-two-month-old Day screeched "Baby!" her very first word. My sister admitted she loved us, "at first." An amateur psychologist, with a BS in sociology at age fifty-eight, I'm sure my sister will agree, as do I, with Arthur Adler's opinion in his book, Theory of Birth Order.

"The firstborn child receives parents' undivided attention, then is dethroned by second-born and must share attention." Adler claimed, *"Favorable outcomes include feelings of protection and care for siblings."* Dare I say my sister acquired Adler's unfavorable outcome those, *"feelings of insecurity, feats of sudden reversals of fortune, hostility, pessimism."*

Once, defending Day against my bad-mouthing, Ma said, "I don't want to hear you picking on your sister anymore. After all, she WAS my firstborn." Feeling as if I'd been doused with a bucket of cold water, I responded in a splay of sibling vindictiveness. My sister and I were at constant odds. I took evil delight in pulling her long golden-red braids and calling her "Bugs Bunny," due to her prominent front teeth. Ma often took me aside and said, "Don't pick on poor Day, she has an inferiority complex." I'm sure it was difficult being upstaged by everyone's darlings, "the twins." There were other things too. Day wore braids until age fifteen, while Ma and Aunt Ethel fussed with my hair, producing curly ringlets. I even had a beauty parlor perm at age five. My sister told me she never liked Aunt Ethel. Once, when she'd gotten up before the rest of us and went over to the Wagners, Aunt Ethel snapped, "You'd think your mother could get up early enough to braid your hair!"

Day often escaped from us twins by visiting Aunts Millie and Rose, where she helped houseclean and earned quarters for her favorite escape, the movies. When Day turned fifteen, Aunt Millie took pity on her and chopped the piglets off. Ma, incensed, kept the thick golden-red tresses wrapped in tissue paper in her handkerchief drawer, which indicated to me a special warmth for her firstborn.

My sister should be consoled by now, realizing I ended up the loser in our hair competition. I'm sure that the curling/pulling/burning with steel rollers, not to mention Aunt Ethel's eye-stretching rag-curlers, contributed to my current thin hair/prominent bald spots. Day, however, has a fine head of hair. In the evil glint of my mind's eye, I picture my sister as a gawky, freckle-faced redhead with waist-long, thick braids, her eyes downcast, lips permanently pouted. My twin's nervous smile is forever lopsided, his small hand shading his eyes. I see myself the star: blond, tousle-headed, with an infectious ear-to-ear grin. A K-Mart associate's guess who baby-picture-contest found me the most easily guessed, thanks to that grin. You would have thought the replaced pearly-whites would have thrown them.

Adler says that the second-born has to share attention from the beginning and that unfavorable outcomes include rebelliousness and envy. Twin Howard became a problem after Grandma Larsen died. He wouldn't go to school, was running with roughnecks and was forced into counseling. Years later, he told me, "They made our dad promise to take me fishing, but he left me at his fat girlfriend's place in the woods and went by himself." Howard chuckled over his memory. The girlfriend, assuming Howard could drive, had him haul some junk to the dump for her. "I had to take her retarded son with me and when I ran off the road, he screamed like a stuck pig!" he said.

In my self-absorption, I figured his problems started when the powers that be in the educational system changed their stance on keeping twins together. Howard and I were separated in sixth grade. After eighth grade graduation, when I lost the American Legion leadership award to my nemesis, the brainy, flat-nosed Doris Raulerson, Howard jeered and poked fun at me, reducing me to tears. Mother's comforting words that I wasn't chosen because she was an active member of the American Legion Auxiliary, could never assuage the pain I felt from his treachery,

Our late, new-found friendship brought the realization that my twin had a fine-honed, though warped sense of humor. Among the bon-mots he used to get my dander up was, "Women were put on earth to bleed and breed."

According to Adler, *"A last-born child has several models, receives much attention, is often pampered. Favorable outcomes include much stimulation and many chances to compete, often outrunning all siblings."*

I literally outran <u>my</u> siblings: the earliest to walk, the first to speak. A favorite story was Aunt Ethel's recital of Howard and me in our playpen: "You'd walk round and round, hand over hand. When you got to your twin, you'd straddle him and keep going. He'd stand frozen, clutching the playpen bars."

On the other side of the coin, Adler's unfavorable outcome possible with last-borns includes feeling inferior to everyone, and the likelihood of becoming a problem child/maladjusted adult, due to spoiling. Adler claims pampered children expect society to conform to their self-centered wishes, want to be the center of attention, fear competition and feel their own position is right, that any challenge unjust. Adler claims we are potentially the most dangerous of all people in society!

Sometime during the 1980s I read an article that refuted my favored position as last born. It lay out a theory that in conception, fraternal twin eggs being separate, the first inseminated is the last born. Alarmed, I discussed the article with company nurse-friend, Miss Waldschmidt, at the bank in Chicago where I worked. The tall, gangly, crisp as her uniforms nurse, called the theory, "Wacko!" I couldn't resist telling my twin, "I've been living a lie, being the spoiled brat all these years, when technically, you're the younger and should have been the star." His response? - "Who gives a shit!?"

Years after, when I'd rushed home for one of the crises that plagued the last ten years of our mother's life, my siblings and I gathered for cocktails after the worst was over. Day and Howard, intent on attacking me during my on-going accusations of their neglect of Ma, insisted, "You were always Ma's favorite." I countered, "You two just made bad choices." Day latched onto Grandpa Larsen, Howard to Grandma Larsen. Grandpa died in 1943 when Day was ten, Grandma in 1948 when Howard was thirteen. Who could know that Ma would live to ninety-one, my favored status to last fifty-two years? During that sibling get-together, I also pointed out that the two of them never were interested in our family history, never appreciated Ma's feelings for us, like when we were infants and she prayed she'd live long enough to see us grown.

Ma said her prayer was precipitated by the fear that overcame her on seeing a funeral procession for a woman who left five underage children, who ended up in an orphanage. At age ninety Ma often wondered aloud why she was still alive. I teased, "It was a curse for that prayer." Ma replied, "You're right. I remember Grandma Larsen wondering why she was still around when she got old. I told HER, 'You're here to help raise my children.' Now THAT was a real curse!"

Our upbringing was an enormous challenge, I'm sure. In

my fictionalized account, I wrote, *"My twenty-five year old la-
borer father basked in the sun of attention produced by the
multiple birthing of his thirty-nine-year-old wife for the next
two years, then abandoned the family. We twins and our sister
were raised on the meager income from old-age pensions, in-
termittent child-support, handouts and public aid."*

My memory teems with Great Depression stories such as
Grandpa Larsen trudging mile on mile each winter to cut wood
for fuel. He trekked a route from Cumming and Stinson Av-
enues out highway 105 to Billings Drive to land owned by Great
Grandpa Waterston, Grandma Oliphant's father. Grandpa Larsen
would saw and stack the wood one day, then return the next to
drag it home by sled. Once he returned to find the wood stolen.

It was said that Aunt Ethel, in spite of a regular income
throughout those years, once ordered a new bed and then got
her money back by insisting it didn't fit in their bedroom. When
the delivery men returned for it, she gave them her old bed.
Two of Aunt Rose's children, my cousins Rosemary and Pat,
told me that they remember lots of hand-me-downs. Their Min-
neapolis maiden-aunts sent huge boxes of used clothing every
Christmas, including a beaver coat that Rosemary hated and
was destined to become mine. Pat recalls a black bowler hat in
one box. He trained himself to roll it down his arm and then flip
it onto his head like Charlie Chaplin.

My unemployed father fished and hunted game for the family. The strain eventually got to him. He left in 1937. It was said
that Grandma Larsen was glad to see him go in spite of the
seventy-five cents a month that his mother, Grandma Oliphant,
contributed to his keep. Grandma Larsen said, "Godt å bli kvitt
ham; han spiste som en hest!" (Good riddance. He ate like a
horse!). And though Ma claimed, "Your grandpa Larsen liked
Damer," I wonder if he wasn't a bit relieved at my father's departure, as well. Aunt Millie, laughing at the memory, related
to me that Damer used to hide Grandpa's nightcap, adding,
"Damer loved to tease that old man." I didn't laugh, immedi-

ately recalling that Grandpa always wore hats of some sort, due to his sensitivity over his thinning hair. Ever jovial Aunt Millie murmured, "Well, I thought it was pretty funny."

Years after, my father said, "Your grandma was a mean, sharp-tongued old lady." In my teens, Aunt Ethel told me, "It's just as well your father left. Every time he hung his pants on your mother's bedpost she got pregnant." I still rankle when I remember those Oliphant utterances.

Grandpa applied for work with the WPA at age seventy-two but was told he was too old. The adults subsisted on tea until a neighbor, noting no one had been out of the house for a week, called the authorities. Forced to go to the hated Relief Department, it was a terrible blow for those proud Norwegian immigrants.

I have no memory of being cold or hungry in those years on Cumming Avenue. Adler theorized that people's earliest memories reveal the genesis of their life style. *"There are no chance memories, we choose to remember things we feel have an important bearing on our life situations,"* he said. Adler also said, *"Life-style is fairly set by age four or five, although it can be changed by purposeful action."* I've spent a lifetime trying to make sense of my earliest memories and their seemingly, self-propelled prophecies:

I see a wheelless panel truck in the backyard, bought for a dollar by Ma as a playhouse for us kids. Howard and I sit on the floor. My panties are down and he's patting mud on my lull'la. Suddenly the double doors fling open, brilliant sunlight frames Grandpa Larsen's dark looming shadow, like a vision of God. The memory abruptly ends.

In the wee morning hours I creep barefoot into the kitchen. I don't feel cold, but know it's cold because the oven-door on the wood stove is down. Ma and Grandma are chatting in Norwegian, sipping coffee. I look up at an empty hole that once housed a stovepipe, see a white mouse peer back and twitch his nose. Years later on relating my memory to Ma, she says it was probably one of father's trained mice, set free when he left.

I'm pulling a miniature sled by a string, a Crackerjack prize. The sled, bright red, makes Lilliputian tracks on drifts of snow. Puffs of my breath, like smoke from an idling steam engine, seep out of the prickly knit scarf wound round my neck and over my nose. I imagine myself on the sled, poised to hurdle down a mountainous peak toward an empty valley below.

Having feigned illness and been kept home from Sunday school, my twin and I jump from behind a door, taunt Day on her return from the long trek alone. As she bursts into tears and runs to Grandpa's arms, we chant, "Cry-baby, cry-baby!"

I'm being held down on the hard surface of an ironing board, with cut eye lid spewing blood. I scream, 'MA-ma!, MA-ma!" Old Dr. Mason leans toward me, needle and thread in hand. My mother gently strokes my head and hums, "Rock-a-bye-baby, in the tree tops..." I drift into sleep.

My siblings and I are hiking to Bethel Lutheran Church; our breath billows in clouds on the cold air, our boots crunch on crackling snow. I look up at the leaden, overcast sky. The dancing Northern Lights dog us, bringing to mind the robed apostles whose pictures grace my Sunday School primer. We near a dark, barren copse of trees. I'm sure trolls and goblins live there, so I press my hand tighter in my sister's hand and lean into her. She nudges me away.

Analyzing my sister's earliest memory is easy. She remembers we had a half-block-long vegetable garden with a flower border. "I loved to pick the flowers there and in our neighbor's yards," she said. On one occasion Ma found her gobbling dirt. To this day my sister has a green thumb. My twin seldom revealed his earliest memories. When pressed, he would say, "I had a rotten childhood, was always cold, always poor."

Many of my earliest memories are inspired by snapshots, lovingly pasted in Baby's Book: blue for Howard, pink for me and white for Day. Most of the pictures were taken with Ma's black box-camera, which she held in one hand, then lowered her head and shaded the lenses with her other hand. All were taken outside and as soon as we heard the dull click of the camera lever, we would stop smiling and disengage ourselves from each other. The developed pictures were pasted onto black photo-album pages with tiny triangular tabs that often dried and fell off. Ma kept the negatives in envelopes that were stuffed into shoe boxes. She always meant to get copies made, but seldom did.

One black and white picture captures my twin and me in a wagon, eyes lowered, index finger of our left hands in our mouths. In another I'm clutching the handle of a pink wicker doll stroller, that index finger firmly in its place. Next to me, my twin grasps the handles of a red wheelbarrow, eyes averted.

Pictures in Billings Park, on the beach at Park Point, my father on the running board of a Ford coupe, holding me on his lap. In another I'm wearing a one-piece bathing suit and clutching a string connected to a white and blue metal sailboat. I can feel the itch of wool on my skin as I peek out from behind my twin. I grin into the sun. I have no recollection of riding in the coupe —no recollection of my father's touch.

From 1933 to 1941 our family lived rent-free at 5420 Cumming Avenue, courtesy of Mrs. Fairfax, one of Grandma Larsen's former employers, in exchange for Ma looking after the property. Ma said, "Mrs. Fairfax was a wealthy woman from 'the south.'" I have her cookbook, <u>Buckeye Cookery</u>, circa 1883, dedicated to, "Those plucky housewives who master their work instead of allowing it to master them." Her delicate signature, "Eunice G. Fairfax," is on the flyleaf, a notary seal on the last page revealing, Tmos. M. Fairfax, Minnehaha Co. Dakota. I also have a picture of Mrs. Fairfax standing in front of the Cumming Avenue house while it was still worthy of its prestigious name, "Fairfax Hall." A symmetrical four-plex, there are three elms in the front yard, a balcony over the columned front porch.

By 1935 the building had lost its charm, porch railings gone, pilings warped, paint chipped, the front yard devoid of trees and grass. In the few pictures of us kids in its vicinity, the building looms in the background, a threatening, dark, clapboard monster. Although details are scrambled, the story of Mrs. Fairfax's demise burns in my memory. She and her daughter died in a bus accident when the vehicle careened through a drawbridge guard rail into a lake. Mother and daughter were found clutched in each other's arms. I imagined it was the bridge between Duluth, Minnesota, and Superior, Wisconsin, though it may well have been in the south. The memory of their deaths was enough to make me snuggle closer to Ma on our frequent bus trips to Duluth over the years.

Details of early friendships on Cumming Avenue remain hidden, but names cling....perpetually smiling and freckle-faced Connie Carlson, sister to the chunky and mean-spirited bully Bonar; he once punched Day in the stomach. In 1982, back in Chicago after the Bryant Grade School all-class-reunion I'd attended, Connie phones me from Texas. I'm in bed, sit up in the dark to listen to the unfamiliar voice from my past. It's an eerie, enjoyable feeling, like waking from a pleasant dream. I'm pleased that she called, pleased to be remembered. Connie lives in California now, and over the years, often asked Bonar about me. Bonar, a community activist and volunteer, died at age sixty-seven on July 6, 1999.

My sister's friend, raven-haired Roberta Weissman, is still in my memory, as well as Janet Lind, ever furtive-eyed and pallid. She lived beyond the Weissman's on Cumming Avenue. Shy, cheerless Frankie Austin, my favorite boyfriend, as I once told Ma is there, and Max, our purebred collie, given to us by the Klear family across the alley because he wouldn't leave Day's side and there was no money to buy him.

The last thing I remember from the Cumming Avenue years is of our first day in kindergarten, September 1940. As Ma attempts to leave, we twins break into hysterical wails. No amount of assurance....Connie Carlson offering a toy, the promise of

graham crackers and milk....can calm us. Ma sits on a miniature chair between us as we nap on rag rugs. I feel the hard
bumpiness of the rug, smell whiffs of stinky turpentine fumes
from fat brushes soaking in coffee cans on window sills.

Things eventually work out, as Ma said, "You were chosen
to be emcee at kindergarten graduation." I remember nothing
of that event.

I rue the fact my early memories are so sketchy, especially
regret my faulty memory when I read Eudora Welty, John
Cheever and other favored authors. I long for their expertise
and genius for embellishing and fictionalizing their recollec-
tions. I especially pine for total recall now - as I move on to the
old Kronlund house, 5926 Banks Avenue, two doors south of
Aunt Ethel. Family records indicate we moved there on April
15, 1941 - a Tuesday.

THE OLD KRONLUND HOUSE

I loved the old Kronlund house. Grandly situated on the north east corner of Banks and Sixtieth street, to me it was a castle. There was a large backyard with an apple tree and a fragrant French lilac bush spread beneath the sun-room bay windows. At the base of the south wall, wild Day Lilies flourished. My sister continuously pulled and whacked at those murderously tough blooms and hates them still. The tumble-down garage loft housed dozens of pigeons. Their constant cooing soothed us on lazy summer days as we kids lolled on the grass nearby. Day recalls, "There was a rickety ladder there that I crawled up to look for baby pigeons. It was hotter than Hades and stunk to high heaven. I remember gagging and being terrified that I'd fall."

We seldom used the Kronlund house front entrance. Instead, we used the side door, entered off a railed porch into the huge kitchen. Empty glass milk bottles were left on the porch for pickup and refills. In winter the milk expanded, pushing up the cardboard bottle caps. The separated heavy cream was a favorite of Grandma's. In summer the milk often soured. I hated the speckled results in my coffee, a brew introduced early to us kids. I trained myself to drink my coffee black.

Grandpa kept the wood box behind the cast iron stove in the kitchen stocked with kindling, resulting in it being the warmest room in the house. He regularly fed coal briquettes to the ancient cellar furnace too, but with less success. Though the registers in the upstairs rooms barely brought an ounce of warmth, they were a joy to us kids. We heard many a puzzling conversation as we crouched over them, ear to the grate, becoming especially attentive when Grandma's excitable voice raised in dismay, "Nei da! Hva skal vi gjøre nå!?" (Oh no, what will we do now!?). Her panic was always abated by Ma's calming words, "Det skal vi nok greie" (I'm sure we'll manage.), followed by whispering so soft it sounded like rustling leaves. We kids would become drowsy-eyed and soon abandon our post for the warmth of our beds.

An oak icebox that seldom held ice was in that kitchen, too. In winter perishables were stored in the pantry; in summer bought as needed. An unused ice pick hung from a nail near the icebox, a tool that once caused much consternation to Grandma Larsen. While entertaining her Norse lady friends, who unlike Grandma, spoke broken English as well as Norwegian, one of the ladies wanted to demonstrate the use of that ice pick as an awl, for re-sizing leather belts. "Get me a pick," she said. Her mispronunciation came out, "pike," a Norse word for the male sex organ. Grandma whooped, "HVA!? Hva sier du?" (WHAT? What did you say!?). The woman was never invited to Grandma's kaffe-klatch again —she probably never learned the reason for her sudden banishment, either.

I vaguely recall the neighborhood ice man passing by. Stooped under an enormous block of ice on his rubber-caped back, water dripped in his wake as he plodded from door to door. Our ice box was a repository for old newspapers and magazines, held in waiting for Ma's scissors. She insisted they be kept for scrapbook material. An inveterate saver, Ma clipped articles on local history, obituaries, recipes, war news, or just about anything that caught her eye. Clip-art, from the magazines was used for we kids' innumerable scrapbooks. Unfortunately, the papers and magazines piled up faster than Ma's razor-sharp scissors could clip.

Those scissors and all other cutlery were kept fine-tuned by regular visits of the rag peddler. Apparently Grandma felt his services weren't as frivolous as the iceman's. The ragman came weekly, propped his knife sharpening machine on the sidewalk below the back porch. The spinning wheel of the whetstone made a soft, whirring sound, setting off flying sparks. It was a ritual we kids never tired of watching.

A massive wood table stood in the middle of the wainscoted

kitchen, protected by a square of black oilcloth. We ate all meals there: Grandpa at the head of the table, Grandma at its foot. Ma and I sat side by side, across from my twin and sister - Howard closest to Grandma, Day to Grandpa. Our days began with homemade donuts, rosettes or sugar-sprinkled and rolled Norwegian pancakes. An occasional Saturday morning treat was Lange's Bakery wine bread, a favorite of the adults.

The kitchen was forever filled with aromas of Grandma's specialties —dark brown gravies, thick white sauces, hearty stews. We had lots of fish too —fried, boiled and sauced, or chopped for chowder. Ma was in charge of hot dishes. Often the windows in the kitchen were steamed over. I spent hours drawing stick figures with my index finger on the panes. Vegetables were ALA Norse —boiled to death, saturated with butter, gravy, or white sauce. Other items, like head cheese, potato and blood sausage, were Grandma's realm, too. I recall a pig's head covered in brine soaking in a crock on the back staircase landing. On a dare I lifted the brick-weighted wood cover to take a peek, screamed in terror at the gory sight.

I often picture Grandma straining gravy through a sieve over her iron frying pan brimming with Norwegian meatballs, a five-star meal to us all. Any left over gravy was reheated and served on bread as a snack. Other snacks were Howard's favorite of sliced tomatoes sprinkled with sugar and mine, of cold bacon-grease on homemade bread, doused with salt and pepper. We ate everything, never turned off by the most obnoxious of fish or onion odors. Herring, Lutefisk, gameløst, Head and Roquefort cheese are perfume to me still. Every meal included dessert -chocolate pudding, Jell-O with real whipped cream, cake, cookies or Norse delicacies. We loved sweets, especially my twin. If there was a favorite dessert like fresh baked apple pie or fig cookies, Howard would tear to the table and shout, "First pick!" It got to the point that every morning my twin bounded out of bed yelling, "I get first pick of whatever's for dessert today!" As hard as I tried, I never beat him. It was said that when we three were in hospital for tonsil removals, as the black rubber ether mask was lowered to his face, Howard demanded first pick of the ice cream we'd been promised. He ended up with all three portions, Day and I were too sick to eat. It's doubly amazing to me now, having learned that my twin was circumcised during that same hospital stay.

There apparently wasn't a specific schedule for all the baking that went on during the Kronlund House years. Whenever the supply got low, fresh batches miraculously appeared. Lord knows how the women managed, especially since sugar was rationed. Homemade cookies and pastries were gobbled off cooling racks before the heat settled. Hot sliced bread was lathered with butter that immediately melted and slid down the side of our hands as we carefully balanced the treat from finger to finger. Most pies were the exception to instant gratification. Baked for holidays or for company, after they cooled, Grandma would yell up the back stairs, "Kom og kjelp meg!" (Come and help me!). Grandpa immediately appeared, stood on a step-stool and as Grandma passed the pies to him one by one, he stored them high on the unreachable pantry shelves. If we kids were still in the room Grandma would put one hand on her hip, then with the other, shake her finger and say, "Det er ikke for oss" (They're not for us.) Our eyes would waver as we steeled ourselves to keep from giggling, anticipating Grandpa's covert wink.

Though required to eat main meals together, they were hardly formal affairs. Ma and Grandma chattered in Norwegian, we kids quietly bandied insults back and forth. Grandpa kept his own council as he balanced peas or carrots on his knife, quickly brought them to his mouth without losing one. He could peel an apple or an orange in one long, curly rope, too. Grandpa's deftness brought awe to my siblings and me. We were excused after we finished everything set before us because, "...barn har ikke mat i Norge" (...children don't have food in Norway). Grandma's habitual admonishment was a waste of breath. We three were all clean-plate-club-members.

Once, as we tossed Ma's antique mesh evening bag back and forth over the still seated adults, it slipped from someone's hands, landed with a plop on Grandpa's plate. Bits of ground meat, elbow macaroni, canned tomatoes and onions from Ma's Spanish Delight hot dish splayed his goatee. Grandma, shaking her fist at us, bellowed, "Nei da" (Oh, no!). Grandpa carefully patted away the mess and continued eating, knowing full well that Grandma would not have tolerated an outburst from him. My Larsen grandparents seldom spoke except for Grandma calling up the back stairs, "Kom og spise!" (Come and eat!). Years later I learned the reason for her enmity.

Grandma never forgave Grandpa for bringing the family to America, blamed her spouse and his brother, "old Pete Gilbertson," for the Larsen's slide into poverty, though once I heard Grandma blame herself. I had crept downstairs to see if Ma was home and overheard part of Grandma's self-accusation, "...som man reder, så ligger man..." (...you've made your bed, now lie in it...). On seeing me standing there looking perplexed, she opened her arms and I crawled onto her lap. Holding me close against her soft body, Grandma drew a deep breath and said, "Ja...barn er fattigmanns rikdon" (Yah...children are the poor man's wealth).

To me Grandpa was a gentle, patient man. Whenever one of us kids told him there was food on his goatee, he'd say, "I'm saving it for later." In his final years Grandpa doted on us grand kids, first pushing Day in her genuine English perambulator, sent by Uncle Gunnar and Aunt Frances from Chicago; later, after Day outgrew that carriage, Howard and me.

Grandpa loved long walks, strolled slowly along puffing on his pipe, hands in pockets or clasped behind his back. Sometimes he would hum the strains of an old Norse lullaby, "Tulla," my mother's childhood nickname. He was always quick to touch his Norse seaman's cap to all who greeted him. I'm sure their respectful, "Good morning, Mr. Larsen," was a balm to his battered spirit. I remember one jaunt with him from the Kronlund house to Central avenue, then west to the train depot where Uncle Gunnar had once worked as a telegrapher. Grandpa held our little hands in his soft strong ones, gently instructing Day to hang on to one or the other of we twins' free hands. Suddenly a giant black steam engine loomed down the tracks, gaining speed as it approached the crossing, blocking out the setting sun. Belched smoke and cinders filled the air, the sharp raucous blast from the steam whistle startled me into hysterical wails. My outburst ended that trip. I often wonder if Grandpa's intention wasn't a nostalgic return to an area beyond the tracks, where a house my grandparents occupied their second year in America stood. Ma once related that Grandma delivered a stillborn child there, a boy, who they had planned to name "Arthur." Grandpa wrapped the child in a blanket, put it in a box and buried it in a field of wildflowers at Riverside Cemetery.

The pantry trapdoor in the Kronlund house was embedded with a steel ring accessing the cellar. Canned goods, potatoes and other root vegetables were there, as well as a coal bin. If I stood on the trap door too long, I was sure it moved, imagined crouched sooty monsters ready to snatch me into the gloom. There were no monsters but there was a rat. Grandma said he was as sly as a "gamle skatteoppdriver" (old tax collector), the ultimate Norse insult. Grandma tried to kill the rat with poison that looked and smelled like peanut butter. She would spread the concoction on pieces of bread, deposit them in kitchen corners at night. The rat devoured the bread crusts but left the poisoned centers intact.

One late night, as Ma and I stood by for moral support, Grandma positioned herself in the pantry, slowly pulled up the trap door and switched off the light. In the dimness Grandma's image, humpbacked, broom at the ready, conjured thoughts of sorcery in my mind's eye. I flinched when she stage-whispered, "Her kommer han!" (Here he comes!). Grandma banged the trap door shut and flipped on the light. The startled rat looked gargantuan. I scrambled onto the kitchen table, Ma onto a chair.

With a whoop Grandma swung the fist-clenched broom overhead and whacked the beast hard. "Herre Guds!" (Holy Gods!), rang out with each whack. The rat soon succumbed. Grandma mercifully covered it with a funeral shroud of tattered rags.

Ma was convulsed in laughter by then. Not understanding her gaiety, I was just relieved the beast was dead. Grandma chuckled a bit, then sank onto a chair. Her typical response of, "Ah vell" (Oh well), punctuated by a quick intake of breath, signaled instant recovery from another disaster of life. We celebrated over coffee, dunked sugar lumps into the hot brew, sucked the sweetness out until the lumps crumbled between our fingers. Somewhere deep inside me I'm convinced Grandma's bravado took root.

A swinging door between the kitchen and a formal dining room was kept closed. I remember a round oak table with matching sideboard in that room. I don't recall the color or pattern, but I am sure a floor length cloth covered the table. Because the room was so seldom used, many of Grandma's oldest treasures crowded the tabletop. Her heavy brown-leather family album, with gold tooled nosegay design, was propped on a metal filigreed stand. Its cover was cracked, small pieces torn loose or lost to time. Once in a great while Grandma would let me hold the book on my lap as I sat at her feet. The pages creaked as I carefully turned them while listening to her patiently repeat the names and relationships of those, her long gone ancestors - "Her er Simonia, min søster, og der er onkel Lauritz og hans kone, tante Karolina. Karolina hadde engelske ben. Lauritz var din bestefars eldste bror" (Here's Simonia, my sister and there's Uncle Lauritz and his wife, Aunt Carolina. Carolina had English (large) feet. Lauritz was your grandpa's oldest brother). Often during Grandma's narrative she would dab at her eyes with a lace-edged handkerchief.

The table held several other old photos on metal stands. I remember one of a young Grandma and her sister, who had died at age sixteen. I would often gaze at Simonia's delicate features and long curly hair. I wondered why such a beautiful young girl had to die. I envisioned her as an adult: she would have been gentle and soft-spoken, the complete opposite of her older sister, Grandma. Another two-framed heirloom held photos of Ma and Uncle Gunnar together and Gunnar as an infant.

There were photos of Grandma's family kirke (church), the two-story house she inherited, its overwrought parlor, all in Larvik, Norway and a print of "The Oscar II," the steamship the Larsens traveled on to America. Whenever she spoke of that trip Grandma emphasized that they had traveled second class adding, "Uff, men jeg var så syk alltid" (Uff, but I was so sick the whole time).

Ma recalled that her brother Gunnar was sick during that entire two-week voyage, as well. She and Grandpa strolled the decks hand in hand, often staggering from side to side with each roll of the swelling sea. A ship's officer, whose cabin door always stood ajar, once offered Ma a piece of fruit from a bowl on a trunk at the foot of his bed. She picked an orange, the very first she had ever seen.

I seldom tarried in the Kronlund house dining room or near that table. The room was always dark, its one window being blocked by the Sands' house next door. It always brought to mind one of Ma's tales of Norway. She recalled as a toddler, when her maternal grandfather, Simon Pedersen, visited their fourth floor Oslo apartment and fell ill. He spent several days lying on a sofa in their dining room. One morning after Grandpa Larsen left for work, Grandma discovered her father had died. She told Ma and Gunnar to stay put while she ran off to get a doctor. Ma remembered her and Gunnar crawling under the table's floor length cloth and peeking out at their pale, unmoving grandpa. Outside, the neighbor's dog, denied entry, was frantically scratching on the front door. Gunnar said it was their grandpa's ghost, trying to get in. "I was so scared!" Ma said.

The dining room sideboard was covered with an ancient Belgian tapestry sent by Uncle Gunnar when he served as a supply-corps Sergeant in World War I France. I was fascinated by its exotic desert scene of robed, mustachioed men on horseback, their heads swathed in cloth. Some stood chatting, staffs in hand, near white-washed, mosque-like buildings. Their camels lazed nearby, loaded with goods, suggesting a bustling market. Two tents in the background, with opened flaps, revealed men sitting cross-legged in a circle. The scene was replete with palm trees and sand. I imagined myself in the midst of that scene, swathed from head to toe in cloth that disguised my gender, no doubt around the same time I heard the story of Mata-Hari and longed to be a glamorous spy.

Though I didn't know it at the time, that enclosed sideboard held shelf on shelf of old treasures. Grandma's full set of Haviland China and chocolate pot was there together with Ma's collections of cups and saucers and salt and pepper shakers. Grandpa, who in the old country drank his coffee with cognac, had a collection of shot glasses that resided in the sideboard as well. Grandma called a halt to Grandpa's drinking their second year in America. Tipsy, Grandpa had entered the wrong door in a duplex they occupied, the good widow there turned him around and escorted him back next door to face Grandma's wrath. Ma told me, "Your grandma did enjoy a little beer on hot summer days. She'd send Grandpa over to Kronlund's saloon with a tin pail to fetch them the foamy ice-cold brew."

The sideboard also held three lead crystal bowls, innumerable mini-salt dishes, wine glasses and wine decanter, eight or nine decorative plates, china and glass vases, egg cups, sugar and creamers, candle holders, candy and condiment bowls, and luncheon sets. A huge collection of eighteenth century silver and silver-plated flatware, wrapped in newspapers, completed the cache. None would see the light of day until long after Grandpa and Grandma were gone.

There was a closet secreted under the front stairway in the dining room. The door was always left ajar for our collie, Max. Often after supper, while Ma and Grandma were busy in the kitchen, Grandpa would secret himself in that closet, throw Max's horsehair blanket over his head and shoulders, then slowly crawl out on hands and knees like a bear emerging from hibernation. We three kids screamed in mock terror as Grandpa lumbered across the floor, intent on seizing us, wrestling us to the floor. We rolled together, laughing and hooting until Max joined in the game, excitably barking as he circled us. Grandma would soon appear and, with hands on hips, head nodding in disgust, would loudly tsk-tsk, step past us and, thumping her cane in her wake, make her way to her rocker. Disentangling himself, Grandpa would quickly retreat up the back stairs to his room.

There were pictures on the walls, though I'm not sure where they hung in the house. I especially recall some eight by eleven sized prints: Gainsburough's *The Blue Boy* and two by unknown artists, *Young Girl With a Robin,* and *The Lone Wolf.* The former was my favorite as it seemed to draw me into its setting of a mysterious blue and green hued forest.

Grandma's Singer treadle sewing machine occupied a corner. She spent hours fashioning hand-me-downs, repairing hems and sewing innumerable aprons from paisley flour sacks. Albeit sometimes late, for birthdays and holidays Grandma made new clothes for us kids. Often one or the other of us was recruited to thread needles, a daunting task as we had to lean close to her. We were in fear we could never meet Grandma's high expectations. Later she hand sewed dance recital costumes for me with me often in tears thinking Grandma would never get through on time. "Don't worry, it'll get done," Ma always said. Grandma was deft at pinning and basting last minute adjustments to those frilly affairs. Pins frequently jabbed as I pirouetted across the stage. We didn't much appreciate Grandma's talents, I'm afraid. I recall how I especially hated Cousin Rosemary's second hand beaver coat, resized for me. It was humiliating to wear to school. I wanted a regular store-bought coat like everyone else. Buttons, hooks, belt-buckles and zippers were removed from unsalvageable clothes and saved in tin coffee cans that smelled of rust. Those collections included items from clothes worn by Ma as far back as World War I. She had learned Grandma's lesson well: "Penger spart er penger tjent" (A penny saved is a penny earned). I lugged a couple cans full of those buttons around for years, finally selling them to an antique dealer in the 1990s for a pittance.

The seldom used parlor housed Ma's piano and ebony lacquered music stand, received by her as confirmation gifts in 1909. Ma sold both in 1956 for five dollars. Though she claimed she couldn't read notes, Ma had a collection of close to five-hundred pieces of pre-World War I and World War I sheet music, donated to the Douglas County Historical Museum in 1994. Ma's musical talent never was passed on to us kids. However, once, after mentioning to my twin that I always regretted I never learned to play, he said, "Me too."

I don't remember Ma playing her piano in the Kronlund house. Grandpa's Edison Victrola, bought at auction, stood next to Ma's piano, silent sentinels of past glory. Neither Grandpa or Ma dared bring either to life, as any reminder of more prosperous days increased Grandma's righteous wrath.

The ivory piano keys were yellow with age; some were chipped, though the lowered cover hid them most of the time. The top of the piano was overloaded with knickknacks and pictures. Among the myriad objects were three figurines that I adored. One was a twelve-inch-long farm boy lying on his stomach, barefoot, with rolled up breeches. His arms were crossed, one hand held the end of a stem of hay, the other end between his lips. The other two were Tyrolien dancers, the males in Liedehosse and feathered hats, the women in long full skirts with aprons billowing out above their ankles. Their long-sleeved blouses were draped with shawls; flat black pancake hats graced their braided hair. The couples, executing turns, clasped their hands above their heads. The men's heels kicked the air. Each intricately carved figurine base was forest green with flecks of gold. The faded and chipped paint on the dancers was once brilliant red, white and green, the patina on all three softened with age. Grandma told me that those artifacts had been purchased by Grandpa in Germany when he and Grandma toured the European continent in 1902, adding, "Ja, Kjøpmenn liker bestefar din ganske godt" (Yah, the shopkeepers liked your grandfather real well).

There were two Greek style cast-iron urns with black marble bases on each end of the piano top, together with one unmatched urn in the middle. The latter urn had a silver-tooled base, handle and spout attached to its hand-painted white marble body. A silver stopper secured the top of that urn. I still have the cast-iron urns, but cringe in agitation when I remember the silver urn. During the 1950s after I'd left Superior, Ma, in dire need of cash, sold some family heirlooms. Amongst them was that unmatched silver urn, sold for two dollars. Not long after, an article appeared in the *Duluth News Tribune*, headlined: **"Rare Find!"** The article reported it was a scarce funeral urn. It's doubly annoying to me now since learning that that urn no doubt held the ashes of Simon Pedersen, Grandma Larsen's father!

There was a mission-style cracked leather sofa and two rickety rockers in the parlor, too. The latter were acquired when Grandpa worked at The Webster Chair Factory, where, Ma said, "Everyone liked your grandpa. He was quite the comedian when your grandma wasn't around." A carpet so faded the design was obliterated, graced the center of the room. Lacquered wicker plant stands held huge mother-in-law-tongue plants. The sliding doors were kept closed, except at Christmas when our live tree graced the front window. During World War II a silk service flag, red and white with a blue star, hung in that window advertising my father's service in the US Army Air Corps.

The middle sun-room, with its bay windows, housed Grandma's oak and leather rocker, next to an oak library table. A fringed cloth protected that cherished piece. In the center stood a cast-iron lamp, complemented by its shade of intricate stained-glass panels. My sister says a cage on a stand next to the library table held Grandma's canary. Grandma adored that bird, loved when it burst into song each morning after she removed its cover and spoke to it in a singsong voice: "Ja men, du er så pen!" (Yah, you're so beautiful!). I remember the bird cage and stand, but not the bird. Perhaps the vision of Grandma luxuriating in pleasure was too perplexing for me to grasp.

Grandma spent any free time in her rocker, eternally tearing strips of cloth for rag-rugs, basting them end to end, then rolling them into large balls while mumbling to herself and breathing deep little gasps of chagrin at some long ago insult. Her hand-sewing was done there, as well. Ream on ream of rick-rack was delicately back stitched on flower-sack aprons. Once or twice a month Grandma sat up after dark, watching for Ma to get off the bus from trips downtown to American Legion Auxiliary and Daughters of Norway meetings. Often times Grandma dozed, but most of the time she was simply doing what she said was, "Vaere på sin post" (Being on guard).

There were *coffee and* gatherings in that sun room for Grandma's oldest friends. Frenetic three-day house cleaning preceded the events. Both Ma and Grandma had piles of projects in collapsing tumbles around their rockers, requiring fine sorting and relocation before the floors were attacked. The rising dust from carpet-sweeping with a dampened broom coated the already dust-caked furniture. Grandpa was excused from the major project of dusting generations of knickknacks and framed pictures that adorned the piano, tabletops, shadow boxes and bric-a-brac shelves, but not my twin. He trailed behind us, constantly whining, "I don't see why I have to help. It's girl's work!"

It was well worth the effort as sometimes we kids were allowed to join the group for coffee and sweets, after the main topic of conversation had been hurdled. While waiting upstairs, ears to the grate above the sun-room, we heard unfathomable whispered phrases of: change of life baby, the curse, and private parts. When summoned, our entrance into the room of elderly women was always accompanied by Grandma's warning,

"Husk, små gryter har også ører" (Remember, little pitchers have big ears). She was unaware that, though we didn't speak her old-world language, we understood every word. My sister, at age five, only spoke Norwegian, and had to be taught English when she started school. I didn't begin my Norse language studies until the 1970s, am at it still. Regret often pulls at my heart strings knowing I never got to chat with Ma and Grandma in their native tongue.

A more frequent visitor to the Kronlund house was Aunt Ethel and occasionally, Grandma Oliphant. The preparations weren't as extensive for them. Grandma Larsen didn't think much of the Oliphant clan and often repeated how, upon arrival for lunch at the Oliphants, there stood Grandma Oliphant dousing her kitchen floor with a bucket of soapy water, calmly sweeping dirt and all out the back door. Grandma Larsen disapproved of Grandma Oliphant's bobbed hair, smoking and her divorce, too. Rumor was that that tragedy was precipitated by Grandma Oliphant's affair with a married man. Aunts Ethel and Rose told me the man was a street car conductor; Aunt Millie claimed he was a surveyor. I like the street car conductor version best, as it lends itself to Grandma's romantic bent. In any case, I learned the name of the culprit in the 1990s and was struck by the similarity to our Oliphant surname, Oliver. He sold Grandma's love letters to her mother-in-law, Great Grandma Annie Elizabeth Oliphant Tongue. Great Grandma Tongue needed something dramatic for her daughter-in-law's counterclaim of accusations of womanizing against Great Grandma's son, Grandpa Oliphant.

In 1997 I got a copy of my grandparent's divorce papers but was disappointed that the details of the case were missing. Grandpa Oliphant won the suit against Grandma, though he agreed to pay alimony of thirty-five dollars a month commencing on November 2, 1934. Grandma was found guilty of: "A course of cruel and inhuman treatment consisting of constantly nagging this defendant, staying away from the home of said

42

parties at unreasonable times and hours and mental violence inflicted on him."

Everyone in the family conceded that Grandma hated housework and left her oldest daughter Ethel in charge, while she sat on the shores of Lake Superior smoking and writing poetry. Copies of Grandma Oliphant's unpublished poetry includes the ode, "On A Streetcar." I remember the first time I read that piece, remember the rush of adrenaline the words raised. To me it was concrete evidence of that long ago scandal and more importantly, brought to me an insight into Grandma Oliphant's spirit.

On A Streetcar
By Grace Darling Waterston Oliphant

Oh, yellow streetcar, clanging thru
the city's busy street,
Your trolley snapping sparks of blue
like stars upon the wires

You bear the busy, rushing throng,
The happy and the sad,
The young, the gay, the old, the lone,
The good folks and the bad;

You take them all where they would go,
Nor count them aught but "fares";
Each but a token means to you,
You heed not of their cares.

Each one a tale of life could tell,
Be it of joy or pain;
You ring your jangling little bell
And count each fair again.

Grandma Oliphant was steeped in Scots culture and whimsy, completely free from the down-to-earth practical stoicism of my Norse grandma. She and Aunt Ethel were vivid story-weavers. Their discussions of Scots history, our shared ancestry, poetry, spiritualism and seance participation were fascinating to a little girl with a big imagination. Grandma Oliphant got a kick out of pronouncing that <u>her</u> forebears called the Viking raids, Norse myths, and that the co-mingling of those ancient tribes was envisioned by many a Scots druid. Their mystical forecasts bore out that the best of the two races would produce a superior North Man, according to Grandma Oliphant. Her favorite example was 1940s film star Greer Garson, forever after inspiring in me a kinship for Greer and her clear, translucent Norse complexion, combined with flaming red Scot's mane. I was convinced that someday I would be just as beautiful.

Grandma Larsen tolerated Aunt Ethel, as she and Uncle Art were we twins' godparents and were instrumental in our upbringing, both financially and tribally. Grandma thought it important for us to become real Americans, though she never acquired citizenship

During one of Auntie's visits, annoyed with what I thought was her incessant babbling, I went into my act. I jumped and skipped around the room and prattled in a singsong voice. My antics increased as, glancing at Grandma Larsen, I detected a flicker of a smile cross her thin lips. Aunt Ethel, exasperated, began to recite, "There once was a little girl who had a little curl right in the middle of her forehead..." Her dirge-like voice continued to the last line, then, in slowly rising tones, Auntie glowered at me and shouted..."When she was bad, she was <u>horrid</u>!"

Shamed and brokenhearted, I edged under the rocker that Auntie overflowed. I sobbed and sobbed and refused to be coaxed out. My twin, on Grandma's lap teased, "Cry baby, cry baby...." His chant was not far off the mark; I often cried at the drop of a hat. Physical pain, teasing, or just a glance of disapproval, could set me off. I think my twin had gotten the notion that my wails were a ploy to attract attention; he especially detested my antics when they drew Grandma's focus away from him.

This time, his action only increased the volume of my howls. The din dislodged Auntie, who mumbled, "That child and her crocodile tears...." and she soon left.

Still I refused to get up, crouched on my knees on the hard floor, softly whimpering. Grandma and my siblings left for upstairs and bed. I could hear Ma in the kitchen clearing cups and saucers. Suddenly the lights went out. Before I could cry, Ma was there. She swept me in her arms and carried me upstairs to our bed. While she tucked me in, I recited my prayers, my sore knees a reminder to exclude Aunt Ethel from my lengthily, "God blesses..."

THE SECOND FLOOR

There were two staircases in the Kronlund house, one off the kitchen, similarly wainscoted. Stacked with the inevitable magazines and newspapers enroute to storage, it was a challenge to maneuver past each heap without creating an avalanche. The seldom used front staircase had oak ornamental banisters topped with melon-sized orbs - accessed from the front, parlor and living room doors, all kept closed. Early morning barefoot races down the front stairs, through slamming doors, then up the back stairs, brought chill updrafts and goose bumps. It also brought Grandma's wrath, expressed in my all time favorite shriek, "Jeg skal slå deg til hodet står fast i veggen!" (I'll beat you until your head stands in the wall!). It was an empty threat —none of us were ever spanked.

Grandpa's bedroom was the first reached from the back stairs. Directly over the kitchen, he spent long hours behind his closed door, playing solitaire or working jigsaw puzzles. I don't recall ever being in his room. My sister says it had a plain wood table fronting the single window and a single bed. I think Grandpa, who may have seemed idle to family and friends, was inwardly exhausted by life's twists and turns. Often he'd say, "There's nothing to be done about it, now..", though not in front of Grandma. Grandpa had meandered along, accepting the cards he was dealt, never doubting that this was the way his life was fated to be. Though he dabbled in barbering in Norway, after his marriage and Grandma's three inheritances, he spent the next couple years prior to immigration, as a bon vivant - going to auctions, taking Ma and Uncle Gunnar on long walks, playing French horn in the Borgermusikken Korps (City music corps) and singing in the local Male Chorus. Ma remembered many strolls with Grandpa Larsen. She would push her favorite doll in a wicker, umbrella-topped buggy that had loose wheels. Whenever a wheel fell off Grandpa patiently chased after it down the paths of Bokeskogen (Birch tree forest). They used to take boat rides on Larvik's Fjord, as well. Ma said she fell out of the boat once, her skirt billowing around her. She floated unhurt until Grandpa towed her in with an oar. On another occasion a whale slowly circled their craft and then swam back out to sea.

Like two of his four brothers and many of his mother's forebears, Grandpa would have made a fine seaman. I wish I could tell him that being Grandpa to us kids in his final years was an honorable calling. My sister and I keep his memory alive by growing bachelor buttons, Grandpa's favorite flower.

The landing, three steps down from Grandpa's room, was across from the bathroom, an uncurtained landing window opposite a window of the Sands' house next door. Shiny-faced and sandy-haired Eugene, the oldest of two boys in that family, spread a story that he had seen me naked there. Forever after, I thought he had a crush on me. The incident could well have been true, in any case. On Saturday nights one by one, my siblings and I would undress in front of the kitchen stove, then streak up the stairs and jump into a waiting tub of steamy water.

The middle bedroom seemed enormous. A double, brass-framed bed filled most of its space. There were four baseball-sized orbs on each bedpost. If I leaned close to them I could see my convoluted reflection. Day and I often slept there, on either side of Ma. We kids took turns sleeping with Ma or Grandma for warmth on frigid nights. The beds were heaped with homemade blankets, some so ancient that they were frayed and ragged. Pillow cases with Ma's delicate cross-stitched flower and bird designs were yellow with age.

Her Bird's-eye maple bureau and vanity were in the middle bedroom, too. Ma had acquired the set as a teen from one of the Eckstrand girls, whose family employed Grandma as a housekeeper. I never tired of watching Ma at her vanity, preparing for meeting nights out. She would fluff loose powder over her face and long neck, then apply two dots of dry rouge and carefully blend them over her high cheek bones. Clear lipstick was applied and the final touch - a spritz of *Desert Flower* cologne. A whiff of that sweet fragrance always triggers a full blown image of my mother at her vanity.

Ma's deftness at fashioning her bare scalp with a turban was fascinating, too. She had lost all the hair from her brow back to her ears after a childhood bout with yellow jaundice. Relating that story Ma said, "Your grandpa sat beside my bed night and day whenever I was sick." Ma's long coffee-brown hair from the back of her head would be brought forward, then hair-pinned in three knots, one each on her forehead and over each ear. Ma carefully adjusted the turban crown so that each puff of hair peaked out, then she pulled the long ends forward, knotted them and secured them inside the side folds. Ma's extensive collection of turbans included soft wool and chamois' for winter, lacy whites, prints and pastels for summer. I thought she looked as elegant as Joan Crawford.

The trinkets, mini-bottles, and pictures on Ma's vanity were a constant enchantment. In the center of the vanity a round mirrored tray reflected dainty perfume atomizers and one or two pieces of costume jewelry that she sometimes forgot to put back in a cedar box banded in metal and secured with a tiny lock. I was especially enamored of a gold colored, green-stoned six-legged spider. Two diminutive butterflies set in red and green minuscule rhinestones were fascinating, too. On occasion Ma would open her jewelry box and show me some of her older treasures, like an ancient sojle (brooch), about which she said, "My tante Marie gave me this when we left Norway. She was a seamstress and never married. I still have a piece of sheet music she sent me once, too."

I remember the wonderfully woodsy aroma that emanated from that box when the lid was raised, remember its pale green silk lining and etched mirror. Most of the jewelry there were small clasps, brooches and lapel pins. Ma's many old necklaces and bracelets were in the small vanity side-drawers, some broken and wrapped in tissue. Ma always intended to mend or restring them, but never did although she was adept at gluing together broken china. I still have samples of her handiwork, like a Victorian white vase she got from Mrs. Fairfax. The yellowed glue is still visible in its infinitely fine cracks.

Two small pictures always graced that vanity, though every time Ma adjusted its oval plate glass mirror to check to see if her stocking seams were straight, the pictures fell over. One was of Uncle Gunnar in his World War I sergeant's uniform. Its silver frame had enameled, crossed French and American flags affixed on top. The other oblong, brown-metal frame held a photo of Ma and her girlhood friend Marie Onstad in front of a lilac bush. Ma said, "The Onstads lived out past the Nemadji bridge on County Road C. Gunnar and I hiked to their place many times when we were kids."

The vanity's matching bureau had six drawers and like most all the furniture in the house, was covered with a cross-stitched doily. Ma told me, "Your grandma and I used to win lots of blue ribbons at the Tri-State Fair for our handiwork." In later years Ma concentrated on crocheting fine lace edging on linen hankies, which were popular presents on birthdays or as get well gifts for friends.

One of the small bureau drawers held boundless samples of her work, all carefully pressed and sorted by color, though her sewing box was a tangle of thread, hankies, thimbles and scissors. The other small drawer held an enormous collection of gloves, including Day and my toddler crocheted creations of white with pink rosebuds and gold with green rosebuds. I have no idea what was secreted in the four other, larger drawers. I do remember a silver-framed seven-by-ten photo of Ma on top of that bureau in a straw hat with an enormous draped brim that shaded her languid eyes. "That picture was taken when I was President of the local American Legion Auxiliary Unit #65 in 1929 and 1930, the only single woman to hold that position," Ma once said.

I was very proud of all my mother's accomplishments, and often repeated them to myself whenever I was feeling inferior or incompetent amongst my peers. One of my high school freshman year compositions titled, "My Best Friend," designates Ma a philanthropist, referring to the bandage rolling she did for the Red Cross during World War 1 and the fashioning of quilts for the disaster fund when Cloquet, Minnesota, burned in 1918. Even though my spelling was atrocious, I earned a B plus for the essay. My English teacher, the bullet-headed, and balding Mr. Jay, wrote, "You would have gotten an A, but unfortunately one of your facts seem off." I had stated that Ma was born in 1869 instead of 1896. Ma was a bit taken aback on parents' night when Mr. Jay shook her hand and drolly said, "You certainly are well preserved for your age."

I remember a lot of books in Ma's room. She never threw away books, a mania my sister and I share. Many were poetry collections such as an 1881 Golden Poems tome, and Bugle Calls, a compilation of Civil War poems. Ma read "The Owl and The Pussycat," "Little Boy Blue," and "Rub-a-dub-dub, Three Men In a Tub," to us from her One Hundred and One Famous Poems. I was particularly fond of a book titled, The Language and Poetry of Flowers, as it had autograph-album verses and poetical quotations for concepts like Goodness, Gratitude, Home, Honor, Joy, Knowledge and Love, themes that Ma, Aunt Ethel and Grandma Oliphant dwelled on during their Sunday get-togethers at Aunt Ethel's house.

I loved to run my hand across the soft brown suede cover of Gunnar's book, The Rubaiyat of Omar Khayyam and the Moroccan red-leather cover with gold-tooled letters on his The Legend of Sleepy Hollow. Another of Gunnar's books that Ma had was a 1922 edition of Photoplay Plot Encyclopedia. She told me, "He sent for that when he dreamed of becoming a scriptwriter," adding, "Poor Gunnar, he always had big ideas that never worked out. He even bought land near Solon Springs thinking he'd make a lot of money. That never panned out either."

Ma subscribed to lots of movie magazines, like <u>Modern Screen</u>, <u>Movie Digest</u>, <u>Hollywood Romances</u>, and <u>Silver Screen</u>. She loved Clark Gable and once said, "If I weren't married, I'd marry him." Her statement brought some confusion to my mind, but I never asked for clarification. Much later Ma told me, "Whenever I'd say I'd love to marry Clark Gable, you kids burst into tears. You were so afraid I was going out to Hollywood." Ma was fond of Dennis Morgan too, though I think this was because he was born in Wisconsin, something she repeated whenever his name came up. Ma had a few of the popular books of the day, like <u>Forever Amber</u>, <u>The Cossacks</u>, <u>Gone With The Wind</u>, and <u>Desert Song</u>, but most were older books with faded covers and broken bindings.

Ma's bedroom walls were adorned with pictures. I remember our kindergarten silhouettes, cut from black construction paper and pasted on white backgrounds. She had a penchant for silhouettes. Besides those three creations there were two small framed silhouettes titled, *The Meeting, and Glad Tidings.* The former depicted a 17th century couple, the gentleman bowing to a lady holding a parasol, the latter a southern belle under a willow tree, reading a letter. A framed calendar with a thermometer inside from Nelson Dairy, displayed a silhouette of a little boy strolling past a picket fence trailed by a little girl pushing a doll buggy. A tiny decoupage French village scene and two-inch scene of Holland in an oblong metal frame, sent by Uncle Gunnar from France, are treasures still. There were several framed poems by anonymous authors, most decorated with hand-painted pansies or roses encircling nostalgic little verses like: "None can take mother's place, none can ever be..., Half so near or half so dear or half so much to me."

Grandma slept in a single, iron-framed bed in a small room over the bay windows. The only adornment in that room was a small framed photo of Ma and Uncle Gunnar and their sheep dog, left behind when they traveled to America. Their outfits were purchased for the trip, both children clothed from head to toe in Persian lamb, Ma's outfit in white with a muff and bonnet, Gunnar's in black with a Cossack hat. Once Grandma let me take the picture down and admire it. When I returned it, she said, "Ja. Jeg hadde pene barn" (Yah, I had beautiful children).

I only remember one other piece of furniture in Grandma's room —Day's outgrown, gold-painted cast-iron crib, stacked with newspapers. Grandma also had some old Norse books near at hand, including Gunnar's textbook, <u>A History</u> <u>of the Norse Kings</u>, and his book of Norse fairy tales; four Norse confirmation gift bibles with each family-member name embossed, were stacked on the floor. I don't recall Grandma reading any of them.

We kids dreaded the nights when it was our turn to sleep in Grandma's bed. Protests were out of the question, even if we whined that we couldn't sleep. Every time Grandma turned, we had to readjust ourselves around the hump on her back, nesting like teaspoons in a silverware chest. Grandma's frequent use of the china pot on the stool at the foot of the bed, not to mention emptying that pot in the morning, added more humiliation.

Grandma earned her cane and humpbacked posture from an unflagging curiosity. On the evening we twins were destined to be born, Grandma was assured she could attend her Daughters of Norway meeting, no doubt at the urging of Aunt Ethel, who would not have appreciated sharing the spotlight with Grandma. After debarking from the bus that icy night, Grandma, trudging down darkened streets toward home, saw a lighted window with the shade up. "En åpen invitasjon til nysgjerrige øyne" (An open invitation to curious eyes), she said whenever relating the story. Craning her neck, Grandma fell and broke her hip and lay for three hours in ice and snow. She always ended that saga laughing, her eyes filling as she recalled her return from the six week hospital stay and Day, not knowing who she was, dragged out all her toys for Grandma to admire.

Not long after I retired to Superior from Chicago, I met Shirley Nelson, who as a young girl, remembered, "The night Mrs. Larsen broke her hip." It was Shirley's mother who rescued Grandma and pulled her into the house. Shirley said it was a miracle her mother hadn't added to Grandma's injuries. The Nelsons were entertaining that night, and Grandma was discovered as the guests departed. I took delight informing Shirley that Grandma fell while trying to see who was present.

The master bedroom over the parlor on the far side of the front staircase landing, was devoid of furniture except for two children's Webster Chair Factory rockers. Too cold for use in winter, in summer it became our playroom, filled with toys, new and old. Many were birthday and Christmas gifts, worn and broken, but never thrown out. Our teeth-dented celluloid rattles, pink and blue, were there, as well as the plaques of our kindergarten hands imprinted in wet clay, dried and painted pink and blue. Day's plaque hung on Ma's bedroom wall wherever we lived. My sister has it still. We twins' plaques were eventually broken, saved in tissue paper next to Day's pigtails in Ma's handkerchief drawer, left for me to dispose of years later.

There were lots of toys in that playroom. A favorite of mine was a melon-sized rubber ball with a Betty Boop face. I loved to bounce it chanting, "One-two-three-O-Leary." We all had paddle balls and blue celluloid pipes, which used soapy water for bubble blowing. Day and I had miniature celluloid lamps. We had jacks, pick-up-sticks, marbles and paper dolls. My pink wicker doll carriage, sans a wheel, was there, as well. Day and my dolls were strewn hither and yon, some clothed, some naked, a limb missing here and there, many eyeless. Howard's toy guns, trucks and airplanes were seldom played with, though he became a gun enthusiast when he grew up. Howard preferred playing with screws, setting them in rows, imagining them as tin soldiers. That activity was of particular interest to the psychologist he was sent to, later. The psychologist theorized that Howard's activity, combined with his antisocial behavior, indicated that my twin was at war with the world. Howard told Ma the psychologist said he was crazy. Ma immediately stopped the visits.

After my tonsil removal trauma, I slept on the floor in that playroom. Hot and feverish, the coolness of the bare hardwood felt like a bed of clover. I woke to find a long cord of coagulated blood hanging out the side of my mouth. My horrific screams brought Ma and Grandma running. Grandma calmly snipped off the cord with her sharpest shears.

My twin claimed I once took my clothes off in front of him and his friends in the playroom and pranced around like a strip teaser. That escapade I don't remember.

I remember the Sands' kids next door —Eugene, Donna and Ronnie. Although Donna was my age, we never were close. She and Eugene resembled each other, with their chiseled faces and sandy hair. Ronnie was a year younger than we twins, with dark hair and delicate features. He was my first boyfriend. A head shorter, Ronnie seemed in awe of me. I secretly preferred Eugene and thought I could make him jealous by being Ronnie's girlfriend. In retrospect that misplaced romanticism seems to have been instituted at an alarmingly early age. I have a clear vision of being under the Sands' latticed back porch with Ronnie. I was eight-years-old and Ronnie was seven. We kissed and rolled back and forth on top of each other while keeping a nervous eye out for intruders.

In 1991 I read that Mr. and Mrs. Sand's celebrated a milestone wedding anniversary. I was surprised to learn Mrs. Sands' first name was Ethel. Adults never were addressed by first names when I was young. It amuses me to realize there had been four Ethels' in the same block of Banks Avenue during the Kronlund years. Besides it being my second name, there was Ethel Sands, Aunt Ethel on the far side of the Sands' house and Ethel Nelson, a Bethel Church stalwart, across the street from Auntie.

I sent an anniversary card to the Sands', together with a long letter and some pictures, to Ronnie's Colorado address, included in the newspaper notice. I never got an answer, confirming my suspicion that the Sands' thought themselves a cut above us. In 1993 an obituary appeared in the local paper reporting Ronnie's death in a hospice. An irony of our crossed paths was that we shared the same 1959 wedding date, this news sent by Aunt Ethel to Chicago when I married Ernie Gabino.

I don't remember Mr. Sands and don't know what he did for a living. I did think Mrs. Sands was mean. She wouldn't let her kids out to play until they'd eaten everything on their supper plates. Waiting outside, I would hear her sharp voice, "Finish your vegetables, or you can't go out!" and think it odd that they wouldn't eat. I never gave up waiting though —anxious for a glimpse of my heart throb, Eugene. Once, at a birthday party hide and seek game in the Kronlund house, Eugene stepped on my face. In order to be closest to home in the sun room, I had lain down just around the corner as the lights went out. Eugene, confused in the dark, jumped right on me. I'm sure the thrill of his closeness assuaged any physical pain I endured.

Our collie, Max, had a fascination for the Sands, too. He and their terrier were sworn enemies. Every morning Max shot out the back door, frenetically barking. The Sands' terrier and Max would snarl and growl as they ran back and forth along the wire fence that separated them; seemingly if given the chance, they would rip each other apart like combative tigers. After the fence came down, they continued their charade muzzle to muzzle, as if the barrier were still in place.

We adored Max, our protector and playmate. A softy at heart, Max was terrified of electrical storms. Whenever a particularly horrendous thunder clap broke, he clung to Ma's side, pushing against her until she led him to his sanctuary, the dining room closet. He would scramble inside and sleep on the floor until the worst was over. Max met a horrible end after eating insecticide from the Room girls' flower garden across the street. He lay on the grass in our backyard, a thunderstorm bursting around him. Knowing his terror, Ma went out and kneeled beside him, cradling Max on her lap until he died. We kids pressed our faces against the sun room windowpanes, our tears mirroring the raindrops forming rivers there.

Closing my eyes, I can recreate the area around the old Kronlund house. I especially remember views out the bay windows on Banks Avenue. The small German Lutheran church across Sixtieth Street was where the Pauls' worshipped. On summer evenings we kids and our friends played tag and hide and seek in its shadow. The church still stands, though vacant and shuttered and surrounded by a padlocked chain-link fence.

The upstairs playroom window looked down on the Room house with its beautifully manicured lawn and flower beds. An enormous fir tree towered beyond the back of that lovely pale yellow house. Ma always referred to the two Room women, Marguerite and Ruby as, "The Room girls," due to their unmarried state. The lawn sloped down to flower gardens between that big house and Paul's, a family with a daughter my age and an older son, just beyond. The Paul house in that same yellow hue, was smaller and set lower as there was no basement. An apple tree centered in front of the Pauls' kitchen window and sidewalks wended between the two properties. Opposite the Room house was the empty field with Howard's friend, Wyman Rude's beaten path distinctly outlined. A clapboard duplex next to that lot was occupied by the Osterich and Chesky families. Mr. Osterich was one of two custodians at the Bryant School. Though his name was pronounced Astrack we always called him Mr. Ostrich due to his prominent Adam's apple. Over six-foot-tall, white-haired and handsome, the old gentleman had a powerful voice and sang solo in the Trinity Methodist Church choir and special Bryant school programs. Mrs. Chesky had two or three grown bachelor sons living at home. As teens my sister cleaned house for her and I baby-sat Mrs. Chesky's granddaughter, Patsy Grey.

The streets were filled with fir, birch and elm trees when we lived in the neighborhood. Many are gone now, the elms victims of Dutch elm disease. Rooms' giant fir succumbed after being struck by lightening, the Rooms forever grateful it missed both their and the Paul's house when it crashed to the ground.

BIRTHDAYS, HOLIDAYS AND OUTINGS

I loved birthday celebrations, counting the days until the big event. We twins' parties were especially exciting as it was an even mix of boys and girls. Our sister's parties were for girls only. There always was a cake served with milk or orange soda pop. We got gifts from the adults in our family, but were usually more anxious to see what our little friends presented. Many times we judged their loyalty by the originality or price of the offerings, though we dared not utter any disparaging remarks over less than welcome gifts, thanks to Grandma's constant admonitions of "Du må holde det inne" (You must hold things to yourself), or, "Du må alltid gjøre vel imot folk" (You must always be kind to people). Ma told me that in the old country Grandma had steeled herself with those precepts against her mother-in-law's constant faultfinding. My grandmother cherished a letter from a niece, who, twenty-two years after the Larsens left, wrote from Norway, "My mother sends her love. She always remembers how kind Tante Laura was to her."

Games like Old Maid and Authors were popular gifts, as well as pencils and cardboard pencil boxes secured with snaps or the always cherished diary. A five-year diary with a lock would be a really special gift. Chinese checkers and other board games were popular, too, though mostly received from adults. I almost bought an old Chinese checker board that I saw at The Depot Antique Store once, but came to my senses when I saw the forty dollar price tag. It didn't even have the colored marbles of smoky black, blue, green, red, yellow and white. Those marbles were what I loved best about the game. I always picked red when we played, Howard played with the black ones, Day with green and Ma with white, though I knew she would have preferred red. Once when I charitably offered Ma the red marbles, she said, "That's okay, I like white. It reminds me of

Lilies of The Valley." She went on with, "Keats was fond of them you know. He wrote, ' No flower amid the garden fairer grows, than the sweet lily of the lowly vale...the queen of flowers." Howard snapped, "Are we going to PLAY or what!?"

Barrettes and other hair trinkets were special birthday gifts, as well as combs, paper dolls, activity and coloring books. My mother always gave us books. In my early years I acquired <u>Little Women</u>, Howard, <u>Little Men</u>. We shared <u>The Bobbsey Twins</u> series, each receiving one book a year until we had the complete set. My sister got the complete <u>Nancy Drew Mysteries</u> series. She's a mystery fan, still.

Ma frequently read to us. Her deliberate enunciation and resonant delivery was no doubt acquired from the elocution training young women of her era endured. We especially loved her poetry recitations. My favorite was *The Owl And The Pussy Cat,* which leant itself well to our mother's dramatic flair. From its first line, *"The owl and the pussy-cat went to sea in a beautiful pea green boat...,"* to its last, "...and hand in hand, on the edge of the sand, they danced to the light of the moon....," Ma's words evoked fantastic and delightful images in my mind of the adventures of that unlikely pair. Any of my attempts at similar dramatic affectation brought my twin's bellow, "MA! She's showing off, again..make her stop!"

We played cards with Ma as well, authors, crazy eights and hearts come to mind. My twin usually won those games, though I think we females subliminally willed it to be so, as Howard was a poor loser. When he did lose we braced ourselves against his predictable tantrum, "You all cheated!," or, "I'm not playing anymore!," when he had a bad hand. He would throw the cards down and sulking, leave the room in search of Grandma. She never failed to pull him onto her lap and comfort him.

On cold winter evenings we were kept busy making scrapbooks. Ma retrieved her myriad shoe boxes of clip art, set them out on the kitchen table with a bowl of flour-paste and wood ice-cream sticks for applying the paste. We twins' 1940 scrapbooks are treasures still, with their magazine pictures of art-nouveau silhouettes, landscapes for every season of the year, animals, naked babies in wash pans or diapered in playpens, in cribs sleeping, at small tables eating, in rocking chairs, on swings. All the babies were pudgy twins. There were clippings of young starlet Deanna Durban and page on page of beautiful flowers of every description. Cosmos, pansies, iris, roses and carnations bloom forever on our scrapbook pages. Little verses, embellished with line drawings were prevalent, too. One, titled, *When I Grow Up,* is decorated with a family of five costumed bears, from Papa, the tallest, to baby, the smallest. It reads: *"When I grow up,' said Tagabo, 'I'm going to be a tailor, a clown in some big circus show or just a common sailor. Perhaps I'll be a baker man with pies upon the shelf, but while I'm just a little bear I'm glad to be myself."*

Besides birthdays, we loved Easter. We each got an Easter basket, a new outfit and new hats. White straw bonnets with mini-straw flowers were popular with Day and me, though if it was an early Easter, the snow would be flying and we had to forego wearing them. One all time favorite hat was a Scandinavian style wool hat that tied under my chin. It had white and red stripes with two red pom poms on top. I received the hat around the time we saw the movie, Bambi. Whenever I wore it everyone called me Flower. One Easter I received a stuffed yellow chicken with red polk-a-dot bonnet and felt beak that I adored. Easter egg hunts were great fun. The large mallow-filled colored eggs were favorites. The parlor doors were slid back for the occasion, most all the eggs hidden in and around Grandpa's victrola and Ma's old piano and music stand.

On Halloween we would go far afield in South Superior to gather goodies. I have no memory of the costumes we wore. My sister says I mostly wore my dance recital costumes. Ma and Grandma waited at home, the coffee pot brimming with boiled eggshell coffee in readiness for our return. We would dump our bags on the kitchen table, then Ma and Grandma picked choice candies for themselves. It was no use objecting, as that only brought Ma's warning, "You'll get rotten teeth and then you'll have to go see Dr. Sunquist." We had all been subjected to Dr. Sunquist and his terrifying drill when we were sporadically sent by the Welfare Department for treatment after one or another Health Day exam at Bryant School. Those periodic visits did not save us; we all eventually acquired false teeth, Howard the first, when he was in the US Army at age eighteen; me at age twenty-one; and my sister in her thirties. I always suspected that we received less than adequate fillings, as they often fell out. I had the same suspicion about the glasses I was forced to wear. To me they were repulsive with their large clear, plastic frames and an even worse humiliation... they were immediately identifiable as welfare glasses. I threw mine away, said I lost them. Content to walk around in a haze, I went without until she scraped together enough money to pay on time for a pair from forever jovial optometrist Cory Mathissen, who, Ma informed me, "was born in Norway, you know."

The apples and oranges we collected in our Halloween shopping bags were put in an old wooden rosemaled bowl for Grandpa. We seldom had fresh fruit at home, so it wasn't surprising that we kids never developed the same fondness for fruit as we did for candy. We all had sweet tooths, so after Ma and Grandma were through with our Halloween cache' we kids battled over what was left.

Christmas Eve was a big event, always celebrated at home. We would be hyper-excited, nervously wondering if Santa would ever come. Though we protested, we were sent over to Auntie's to see their tree. Like Grandpa Larsen, Uncle Art was in charge of tree trimming. His adroitness at applying one strand of tinsel at a time amazed us. We never tarried long there though, rushing home in hopes of catching Santa. Grandpa would call from the parlor, then slide open the doors. The towering Spruce or Norway Pine, carefully selected by him the week before, would burst into light, gifts spewing out from under its boughs with cards signed, *from Santa*, in Ma's handwriting. We kids would be disappointed that we missed the old gent, never quite understood how he could come and go in such a rush. Our momentary distress quickly abated as we shook and squeezed as many packages as possible before Grandma called us to supper. One year when Max was still alive, as we clapped in delight at the sight of the tree, it began to wobble and crashed to the floor. Max, asleep behind the tree, had heard our voices and bounded out barking in welcome. Grandma's "Herre Guds!" rang out, spitefully directed at Grandpa for forgetting to anchor the tree. As usual, Ma calmed Grandma in Norse, warning her, "Don't spoil it for the kids."

After the showing of the tree we trooped into the kitchen for the traditional Lutefisk supper with boiled potatoes swimming in melted butter topped with dry mustard, preceded by Grandma's short, curt, once-a-year blessing, "Takk for alle Guds gaver" (Thanks for all God's gifts). There hardly was room for Norse desserts of Fattimand and Sandbakkels with rice pudding or Rommegrørt, but we managed to get everything down.

If our boisterousness wasn't quelled by the end of the meal, Grandpa eased into a rocker, lit his pipe and gathered us kids around for his recitation of our favorite Norse fairy tale, *Three Billy Goats Gruff*. Grandpa was especially adept at inflecting the voice of the troll and the hoof sounds of the biggest Billy goat. Grandpa's, "tromp, TROMP, **TROMP!**" sometimes even brought a furtive smile to Grandma's face.

Unlike most Norwegians, gift opening was left until Christmas morning. It was then that we kids thundered downstairs before the sun rose, Max barking at our heels, Grandma shouting for moderation with her, "Hold deg rolig!" (Keep quiet!). We ripped away wrapping paper, anxiously looking for toys and trying not to show our disappointment with the socks, underwear, scarves and other practical gifts that were inevitable offerings from the adults. Our filled stockings were emptied last; we knew they contained popcorn balls, candy, fruit and mini trinkets. The long-woolen socks were mismatched castoffs of Grandpa's, unlike the expensive, fanciful items of today.

After the hullabaloo subsided at home, we were dressed in our Christmas finery and together with Ma, went over to Aunt Ethel's for Christmas dinner. Grandma and Grandpa Larsen never attended those gatherings. Besides Aunt Ethel and Uncle Art, Cousins Barbara Rose and Buddy and Grandma Oliphant, sometimes Great Grandma and Grandpa Waterston would be there. In my eyes, the Waterstons were as ancient as the trolls Grandpa Larsen spoke of. Extremely devoted to each other, Great Grandma, looking as delicate as a Victorian figurine, sat close to her husband, leaning her head of perfectly waved milky hair against his shoulder. Great Grandpa's hair and bushy mustache were swan-white, bringing to mind Mark Twain.

Cousin Barbara and Aunt Ethel would be rushing from kitchen to dining table carrying traditional American fare of turkey and gravy, sweet and mashed potatoes, one or two bowls of vegetables, usually rutabagas and corn. We would find our seats around the overloaded table, then wait while the eldest present said grace. Great Grandpa Waterston and I vied for the skin and fattest part of the turkey, a penchant I still have.

Gift opening followed the meal, a far more sedate ritual than at our house. Uncle Art passed the gifts one by one, we kids in nervous expectancy by the time our packages were received. My sister and I got a doll from Aunt Ethel and Uncle Art every year until we were eleven or twelve years old. And though that seems excessive to me now, Uncle Art worked at the Shipyards during World War II, so the Wagners probably could afford to be generous. I only remember two of those dolls. One was a large ballerina in pink tutu, another clothed head to foot in a red-knit snowsuit with red shoes attached to mini skis. Those shoes and skis reposed in Ma's handkerchief drawer into the 1980s. I don't think it had as much to do with nostalgia as it had to do with the color; red was Ma's favorite hue. The very first doll I ever received was made of celluloid, permanently on hands and knees and when wound up, crawled forever. Two inch twins in pink bunting reside in my memory. I came across their clone one summer at an antique display at the Tri-State Fair in Superior. Suddenly saddened, I confusedly wondered how MY dolls ended up there.

The Wagner Christmas celebration ended with the serving of coffee and homemade pie. I especially loved Auntie's pecan, mincemeat and pumpkin creations and needed little encouragement to have a taste of each.

We spent other special occasions at Aunt Ethel's. I remember the sixtieth wedding anniversary party for my Waterston great-grandparents in April 1942. Great Grandpa was a first generation American, but spoke with a hint of his immigrant father's burred R's lilting from his lips like music. He had a laconic manner, used strange-to-my-ear words, like lassie and laddie and wore white cotton gloves on his arthritic, chapped and crusted hands. Great Grandpa Waterston enjoyed the spotlight, evoking a special kinship in me for that. I remember the twinkle in his eye as he related ancient Scot's beliefs like, "Don't kill a spider or you'll bring on the rain," and "Don't put an umbrella indoors or lay it on a bed," both for the same reason. To my great amusement, he recited a ditty that allied cutting toe nails to days of the week: "Cut them on Monday, cut them for health; Cut them on Tuesday, cut them for wealth; Cut them on Wednesday, cut them for news; Cut them on Thursday, a new pair of shoes; Cut them on Friday, cut them for woe; Cut them on Saturday, somewhere to go. But never, never cut them on Sunday, because that makes the wee fairies cry." He also ventured into the Scottish folklore realm of ghoulies and ghosties, but was quickly cut short by Great Grandma's protest, "Father! You're scaring the living wits out of the wee ones!" Though I'm sure I showed off on that special day, my sister was the one spoken of for years after. She asked our great grandpa, "Do you have hair on your legs?" He pulled up his pants leg to prove he did.

Photo album snapshots indicate that those Wagner family gatherings weren't as frequent as I imagined. There were lots of other special activities, though. Picnics and hikes with Ma, Aunt Ethel and sometimes, Grandma Oliphant were frequent in summer. We would bus to Duluth to the Zoo, Lester Park, Park Point and Duluth's Canal Park. I don't know when Aunt Ethel took up driving, but do remember being in the back seat with Howard and Day at Pattison Park south of Superior, when Auntie tried to turn the car around. Its wheels spun in the sand, the car sliding toward the Falls gorge. Our screams, "Auntie, don't kill us!" must have been unnerving. Back in our neighborhood Auntie turned into our alley and the front wheels got hung up on a culvert. We kids jumped out and ran into our house, never to ride in that car again.

On one occasion we loaded Howard's red wagon with picnic supplies and hiked out to Billings Drive up Central Avenue past Riverside Cemetery. Somehow or other Auntie and Ma managed to pull the overloaded wagon through heavy undergrowth down a steep hill to one of the many inlets on the Pokegema River. That arduous hike, plus the cooking and fussing they always did, left the women exhausted. They dozed off on blankets spread beneath a thicket of birch trees. We kids kept ourselves occupied roasting marshmallows on the dying embers, splashing in the muddy water, chasing butterflies, collecting May flowers and generally entertaining ourselves. The women awoke as dusk was falling. They quickly gathered up our gear, doused the fire and shrieked, "Get a move on!" By the time we got up the hill from the river it was pitch dark. I remember my utter terror at being unable to see ahead of me, reminded no doubt of the ghoulies and ghosties Great Grandpa Waterston spoke of. Ma and Auntie urged us on as we nervously hied past Riverside cemetery, assuring, "There <u>aren't</u> any ghosts or goblins! They're only around at Halloween."

Riverside cemetery was a favorite hike destination during daylight hours. It was there that I first saw Ma and Aunt Ethel smoke. I was quite startled by the sight. Though I was used to seeing Grandma Oliphant smoke, Ma and Auntie never pursued that habit in public or in front of the family.

After they found their favorite spot, a granite bench set behind an obelisk of some noted Norse family, they settled in. Auntie retrieved two Lucky Strikes, wrapped in tissue from her coat pocket and, gently unfolding the paper, proffered one to Ma. They lit the cigarettes with a farmer's match extracted from its large red and blue box, awkwardly holding the cigarette between their thumbs and index fingers. I thought they looked silly as they took quick little drags, followed by immediate ejection of puffs of smoke. They most certainly didn't look like the sophisticated smokers I was used to seeing in movies starring Joan Crawford, Greer Garson or Lana Turner.

After Auntie and Ma finished their cigarettes we would tag behind as they sauntered along reading names off old family headstones and exchanging long ago stories about the families they remembered. We kids would soon be running helter skelter, careful not to cross the grass covered mounds to avoid Ma or Auntie's shriek, "Don't run on the graves - it's bad luck!" Often we would troop up the road to the Jewish cemetery next door. I loved to look at the photos that graced most all the gravestones there, then too, we didn't have to worry about stomping on the graves as there was little space between the stones.

If it wasn't too late in the day we sometimes trekked back out to the highway and up a hill to the Catholic cemetery, Calvary. Ma never failed to repeat stories of Uncle Gunnar and her: "We'd ski out to Calvary from our house on Central Avenue, or slide down the hills there. After, we'd build a fire and roast potatoes under the hot coals." Ma also talked a lot about the Pokegama River, "It was so high in those days, Mr. Kronlund could sail his thirty-passenger cruiser all the way up the river from Billings Park." She'd add, "The boat was named 'The Ethel K' for his daughter, now Ethel Nelson."

One memorable bus trip to Duluth was when Ma and Aunt

Ethel and we kids went to see Cousin Barbara Rose record a commercial at a radio station. She sang alto with The Rex Trio, Rex Beer Company, their sponsor. I don't remember the performance, but remember that Howard tore the new long blue pants Grandma had made for him. He ran along a brick fence that surrounded Duluth City Hall, slipped and got hooked by the seat of his pants on a nail. Ma and Aunt Ethel secured the tear with safety pins.

I remember Grandma Larsen and Ma chuckling over the name of the trio, but didn't understand their amusement. Cousin Barbara Rose was thought to be scandalous for working as a waitress in Virginia's Tavern. A snapshot of her in front of that establishment, with just the first six letters, VIRGIN, visible above her head, caused lots of teasing by the adults.

To me teasing was as bad as physical assault. My defense, "Sticks and stones will break my bones, but words can never hurt me," seemed a weak defense. We kids suffered the inevitable Elephant phase by our tormentors. A generation later my twin's three children suffered the same torment. After my friends, Lois, Doris, Donna and I shared our middle names of Lena, Selma, Mae and Ethel respectively, Doris and Donna teased me by holding down their tongues and pronouncing mine. The result, "ath-ole" brought gales of laughter and sent me home wailing. My sensitivity always brought tears, assuaged by skeleton in the closet stories from Ma and Grandma. They would ask who the guilty party was, then launch their defenses: "Doris shouldn't think she's so smart, her mother mops floors for a living..." "as for Donna, her mother doesn't even know how to sew!" "Neither one of their families have anything to brag about as far as I can see...." Never mind that Grandma had once been a housekeeper, never mind that for the life of me I never could learn how to sew rick rack on aprons. I lapped up their sagas like a kitten with a saucer of cream and like them, became a repository of secrets, an irrepressible story-carrier.

Aunt Ethel and Grandma Oliphant shared those gifts, as

well. The Oliphant defense included stories of heroic Scots-
men, coats-of-arms, bravery and wealth. The problem was that
I sometimes got facts confused. Once, after Grandma Larsen
spoke of her presence on the dock in Larvik, Norway, waving
at Fridtjof Nansen's exploring vessel, Fram, setting out on his
search for the North Pole, I peddled the version of Grandma
waving to Leif Erickson on his way to discover America. I
bragged a lot about my Norse ancestors, which sometimes back-
fired. When I spoke of my granduncle, Grandpa's second brother,
settling in Africa and marrying a mulatto, Doris said, "You do
look like you've got Negro blood."

I bragged a lot to Doris about my closeness with my
mother, too. She challenged, "If you're such good friends, ask
your mother what a prostitute is." I ran home, the question
tumbling off my lips before the door slammed behind me. Ma
cautiously asked, "Do you know what a house of ill repute
is?"..."Do you know what a lady of the night is?" My noes
brought the disappointing response, "You'll just have to wait
until you're a little older." Back with Doris, she admitted she
didn't know what a prostitute was, either. We searched in vain
for the word in her mother's dictionary. During puberty I suffered horrendous acne. Doris insisted I had syphilis!

Ma thought Doris was a bad influence on me. I thought
her brilliant, though secretly I believed she wasn't as pretty as
me. For one thing her nose seemed too fat for her face and her
lips were puffy and uneven. And though we argued incessantly
about the subject, I was convinced her legs were skinnier than
mine. In my heart of hearts I was sure the Raulersons were better off than us. Doris was allowed to wear grown-up jewelry,
for one thing. I coveted a black onyx ring with a tiny diamond
chip in the middle that she wore. Once at Aunt Ethel's, I took
Cousin Barbara Rose's rhinestone bracelet off her dresser. I
would wear it to school, then remove it before I arrived home.
One afternoon I forgot I had it on when I stopped at Aunt Ethel's
on an errand. She nonchalantly commented, "Gee, that bracelet

looks just like one Barbara has." I immediately excused myself to go to the bathroom, raced upstairs and returned the bracelet to my cousin's dresser.

Doris got us in hot water on several occasions. When we belonged to Mrs. Jacovetti's Girl Scout troop we would do impressions of women gossiping. Our petite, bubbly scout leader bawled us out for being disrespectful. Another time after a troop meeting, Doris and I hid in the school, sneaked into our classroom. I stood guard while she rifled our teacher's desk looking for the results of a recent exam. We weren't caught, but later when Doris won the American Legion merit award, I wished we had so that everyone would know of her dubious integrity. I never considered myself liable.

The most monstrous of our antics was the guess who show we put on for Doris' sister, the Elizabeth-Taylor-look-alike Vivien; and my sister and their friend, tall, gangly, Betty Hannum. Doris, Donna and I were the participants as far as I remember. The performance was held in the Raulerson apartment, with the three elder girls primly perched on the Raulerson sofa. We youngsters went into the single bedroom, stripped and put paper grocery bags over our heads and paraded out one by one as Doris announced, "Guess who's who!" My sister shrieked, "I'm going to tell Ma!" then ran from the apartment with Betty. Vivien took it quite well, saying it was easy to guess Doris, "She has the skinniest legs!"

After high school graduation Doris took off with two other classmates and traveled around the states, eventually settling in New York City, where her sister and mother had relocated. There Doris met and married a lawyer, had two children. They lived in Shelton, Connecticut. Her cousin once told me that Doris used to have her mother serve at parties wearing a black and white uniform. My brother bristled when I told him that story, insisting that maybe Mrs. Raulerson <u>wanted</u> to help. I suspected Howard's defense harked back to the childhood crush he had on Doris. I saw my nemesis at a couple high school reunions over the years, recall that whenever she was in Superior Doris, by then sophisticated, svelte and expensively clothed, harangued about the provinciality of the place. Later reunions when she, like many of us, were high on alcohol, her cousin said Doris was probably on pills, too, the result of her divorce.

At the thirty-five year reunion in 1988 Doris called me late one night, wanting me to come down to the bar at Barker's Island Inn, where I was staying. I declined as I had forgotten to bring a head-scarf and didn't want to go out with my hair in rollers. The next day I saw her at the high-school building tour. I was in a rush to catch a cab for my hair appointment so didn't stop to talk. She ignored me at the evening banquet. In the fall of that year Doris died suddenly. Her passing haunts me still.

"Snooks," Other Friends,
World War II and "A Fine Fix"

The first week we occupied the old Kronlund house, I stood with Aunt Ethel on the public sidewalk opposite our back porch. I had probably whined that I didn't have any friends in the new neighborhood. Auntie pointed out Lois Paul's house, a block away, "Why don't you go over there and make friends with the little Paul girl? They're real nice people." Besides being too shy with strangers to make such a move, I wasn't sure which house Aunt Ethel was pointing at, thanks to my astigmatism, undetected at the time. Lois and I eventually did begin our lifelong friendship, exchanging Christmas card updates to this day. I thought Lois was beautiful with her dark hair, ivory skin and blue eyes, so different from me. She suffered from water on the knee as a youngster, now is wrought with arthritis, one of the reasons for relocating in Arizona. Lois married a football hero after high school, had two boys, and is now retired from her school cafeteria manager job, her husband from his football coaching duties.

Lois and I were hooked on paper dolls; our collections would be the envy of antique dealers today: June Allyson, Linda Darnell, Bette Davis, Deana Durbin, Judy Garland, June Haver, Rita Hayworth, Sonia Heine, Dorothy Lamar, Lana Turner. We made paper dolls from Sears and Roebuck catalogs too, creating whole families by cutting out their forms, then pasting them onto cardboard. Ripped pages from sample wallpaper catalogues were a favorite source for fashioning paper doll clothes.

My 1943 grade-school autograph book has Lois' message: "You look like a little pig, just like me. A pig, Lois Paul...your next door kid." I suspect Lois wrote that message around the time we had a spat, probably over something we were playing, which besides paper dolls, included house and school. I always insisted on being the teacher as the easel black-

70

board was mine. I remember walking with Lois on the path between our lilac bush and the bay windows one early morning. My arm across her shoulders, without warning I put out my foot, tripped her and threw her to the ground. I carried the guilt for that act for a long time after, as, glancing up, I saw Grandma in the bay window shaking her fist at me.

Lois and I played dress-up, clonked around in the discarded brown/white and navy/white spectator pumps of the popular, vivacious Tyson twins, Cousins to the Sands.' I remember Lois once whispering in awe, that her brother Donald, "...is dating one of the twins, maybe both!" We put on shows on our front porches, with clothesline cord strung across, a blanket for the stage curtain. By then we had included Donna Sands and Doris Raulerson in our circle. Doris and her sister lived with their mother in an apartment building a half block away on Tower Avenue. Their dad had died of tuberculosis. Though my sister remembers him, I don't. To me it was perfectly normal that they didn't have a father.

I remember Lois Paul's father Ben well. He called Lois "Snooks," after "Baby Snooks," a popular radio show. Her family nickname, like mine of "Sweetie," was never used outside our homes. Tall and lean and forever clothed in dark, conservative suits, Ben Paul worked across the bay in Duluth, Minnesota, in the office of the Soo Line Railroad. My sister recalls a quarantine sign posted on the Paul's front door for one or another childhood disease. In order to continue working, Mr. Paul had to find living quarters away from home. He could often be seen standing on their front porch talking through the screen door to Mrs. Paul. Lois recalls that once during that quarantine my mother left a plate of fudge there for her. Lois still has the plate.

When Lois and I played paper dolls in a corner of their kitchen floor with Mrs. Paul busily getting supper ready, Mr. Paul's return was the signal for my departure. To me Mr. Paul was happy-go-lucky, always had a friendly word for me, *"Are*

you still the star pupil at Bryant?" or, "How's our favorite ballerina?" One afternoon on his return from work he grabbed Mrs.
Paul around the waist and pulled her onto his lap as he sat down.
Mrs. Paul shrieked, "Not in front of the girls, Bennie!" I was
overcome with embarrassment.

Mrs. Paul seemed stiff and straightlaced. Dressed in
starched cotton dresses and full apron, her black ringlets always in place under a hair net, she vacuumed, dusted and cleaned
daily. Lois and I were not allowed to play anywhere but the
back shed except in winter or when the weather was bad. Then
Mrs. Paul relegated us to that spot on the kitchen floor in front
of the sink with her perpetual admonishment, "Don't you girls
make a mess, now."

Once when I slept over, while lying in the dark whispering and giggling with Lois, I inadvertently farted. Lois insisted
I go to the bathroom then and there. Besides being surprised
and hurt, I was afraid to go down the dark hallway past her big
brother Donald's closed door to the bathroom. Like our cellar,
closed doors and darkness brought the fear of being snatched
into oblivion.

The Paul house was always spotless. I often felt uneasy
there, as if it were too good for me. Tight chenille bedspreads,
polished floors, gleaming windows, it was so different from my
home. I felt uneasy playing inside, too. My uneasiness in Mrs.
Paul's presence was doubled by my suspicion that she was nosy.
It seemed like Lois' mother was always pumping me for information about my family. Once she asked me where my father
was then said, "Is your mother divorced?" I didn't know what
divorce meant. It was my first inkling that we maybe weren't as
good a family as we should be.

Though my uneasiness in Mrs. Paul's presence persisted,
it never dampened Lois and my friendship. We continued spending hours in play and later, daily walks back and forth to grade
school. Summer twilight's in the early 1940s found many of us
kids gathered on the back stairs of the apartment building where

Doris and Vivien lived. Two sisters, Clarice and Evadne Noeth, lived in one of the four apartments on the second floor. The sisters were complete opposites. Clarice was bland and thin, Evadne stocky and dark, with a bulldog look about her. It crossed my mind that it was peculiar they didn't look at all like sisters, so I decided one was adopted, a term that was being passed amongst my cohorts like juggled bowling pins.

Clarice regaled us with ghost stories as we huddled at her feet. I was especially gripped with terror by her tale about twins alone on the second floor of a dark mansion with a demented killer loose in the area. A sound downstairs sends the bravest twin, a boy, out to investigate. The twin left behind soon hears footsteps...slowly...step by step...creak by creak. Clarice was always intent on dragging out the scariest parts of her recital. The twin advances up the stairs into the room. His sister reaches out and feels a sticky substance on her hand —it's her beheaded brother come back to warn her. They find them the next day, the boy dead, clasped in his sister's arms, she completely deranged. By the time it got dark and we kids heard Ma or Grandma calling us home, we would be filled with panic, race as fast as we could to avoid the maniacs and demons that Clarice spoke of.

Howard's friend Wyman Rude, played at our house frequently. A shy, nervous boy, he spat on his hands, then rubbed them together endlessly. His path through a vacant lot from two blocks over soon became a main thoroughfare for one and all. Wyman's family moved to Amery, Wisconsin, before we finished grade school. Because they were of fine Norse stock, Ma kept up a correspondence with Wyman's mother for some years after and learned that Wyman became a druggist.

Other children who disappeared from our horizons during our grade school years were Sylvia Bitney and Janet Lind. I recall going to birthday parties at both their houses, long treks for a small girl in those days. Sylvia lived about ten blocks west of us in Butler Park. I can still see her house in my mind's eye, but not her or the party. Janet lived in our old neighborhood, beyond Connie Carlson's house on Cumming Avenue. Though I have no idea what happened to Sylvia, I remember the tragedy that caused Janet's disappearance. Her alcoholic father was killed by a shotgun wound, supposedly executed by Janet. Rumor had it that Janet's older sister and mother framed Janet and that the sister became a nun. For some time after that scandal I dreamed Janet was an adoptee, victimized by an evil stepmother and sister. In my young mind I felt I always knew she would come to a bad end though, based on the fact Janet was the only one of my girlfriends who never shared her candy bars.

My memories of the war years brim with patriotism, a given. Besides our father in the Army Air Corps, we had two uncles and three cousins serving. I thought they all were very handsome. Teenage cousins Jim and Pat Mockler were in the US Navy, as was Uncle Fred Oliphant. Cousin Buddy Wagner was in the Army Air Corps, Uncle Robert Oliphant in the US Infantry. I only remember seeing my father once during the war, though we had pictures of him in his uniform. He visited while on furlough. I was unusually timid with him that day. When he grabbed me without warning and began tickling me, the roughness of his khaki uniform felt like sandpaper on my cheek. I burst into tears. On that same day my twin and I stole a nickel off the sewing machine cabinet, claimed we had found it while collecting rocks. I don't remember our father giving us money.

Once when Cousin Buddy was on leave, he came up behind me while I was walking down Sixtieth Street. Buddy, a giant of a young man over six feet tall, wore size thirteen shoes. He whacked me on the small of my back and bellowed, "Shoulders straight! Chest Out!" I ran home in terror, positive I had been attacked by a stranger.

We saw a lot of Saturday afternoon matinees —mostly war movies, which I recall as being more heroic than tragic. The actors killed in Hollywood-staged battles never seemed to bleed, or, if they did, it was impossible to detect in the black and white films. We did cry for William Bendix, John Hodiak and other favorites as their life ebbed away in long gasping speeches. My all-time favorite movie was *The Edge of Darkness,* with Anne Sheridan and Errol Flynn as brave resistance fighters in Norway. When my twin and I played war I often recreated scenes from that movie, dropping to my stomach behind a tree and shouting, "Die, you Nazi swines!," then "ack-acking" the sounds of machine-gun fire.

Once when Howard and I went to see, *Reap The Wild Wind,* a Cecil B. DeMille period piece, I blushed in mortification and slid low in my theater seat at the sight of Paulette Goddard's uplifted and half-exposed breasts. On another occasion someone smelled smoke and suddenly the rush was on — screaming grade-schoolers trampling for the exits. My sister made Howard and me sit calmly, our sweaty hands clutched one each in hers. Luckily it was a false alarm.

Years later during one of her visits to Chicago, I took Day to some pseudo intellectual film wherein her incessant stage-whispers were impossible to shush. When she whispered, "Excuse me for bothering you, but I think I smell smoke." I told her to shut up. "Fine," she said, "Don't blame me if we die." Suddenly flames shot up from a trash bin next to the stage. An employee rushed forward with a fire-extinguisher. Day and I left in silence, I unable to bring myself to apologize to her.

Grandma Larsen kept up with war reports in her paper, *News of Norway,* a Norwegian government-in-exile publication. Tears filled her eyes as Grandma read of the terrible doings of the Third Reich occupation forces in her homeland. When we heard on the radio that the Russians had entered the war, everyone except Grandma was sure it would soon be over. "Du kan ikke stole på de menneskene" (You can't trust those people), she bemoaned. Grandma said the same thing about the English, though. She had been an avid follower of the royal families of Europe all her life, so perhaps in that glut of tangled affiliations there was a clue to her proclivities.

War toys were popular and most children could identify the various aircraft, including me, though today I can't identify one car from another. Howard had an enormous green and orange metal Flying Fortress, a plane on which our father flew rear and sometimes belly gunner. Ma took the toy plane to an American Legion luncheon where famous ace Major Richard I. Bong spoke. Unfortunately the Major found it impossible to scratch his autograph on the metal, as requested. Major Bong was a farm boy from Poplar, Wisconsin, a small community east of Superior. Whenever he was on leave he would fly over Superior in his P-38 and everyone would run out to watch him dip and spin overhead. One of his sisters lived nearby and a story spread that Bong once zipped his plane under her clothesline.

We kids and our friends had several ditties that we monotonously droned in singsong tones like, "Whistle while you work, Hitler is a jerk, Mussolini pulled his weenie, now it doesn't work!" or, "Tramp, tramp, tramp, the boys are marching, there stands Hitler in the door...if I ever get a chance I will kick him in the pants and there won't be any Hitler anymore." During the Truman-Dewey election campaign, a mystifying joke circulated amongst us kids: "You can tell how a woman's going to vote by lifting her skirt to see if she's Dewey or Harry."

Everyone saved grease in coffee cans, took them to the butcher or Selden's or Holterman's Grocery, when filled. Grandpa Larsen saved tinfoil from cigarette packs and gum wrappers, rolling them into a huge ball, as instructed. Grandpa, and later, Day, always tended a Victory Garden, as well. Stamp day at William Cullen Bryant grade school still brings a twinge of agony, recalling the urge to hide my face when called on, knowing I didn't have the quarter needed to buy a stamp and make our classroom one hundred per cent.

Those early years in the Kronlund house seemed cocooned in happiness. We kids were fairly healthy except for the usual childhood diseases like measles and chicken pox. I remember a stir of hysteria during a polio scare resulting in the wading pool in Webster Park being drained. Few major accidents interfered except for a near-tragedy my twin and I kept secret. He fell into a deep excavation hole near the front porch. I remember lying on my stomach and stretching my hand down to him. It must have been in the spring, as the ground was hard, the red clay walls of that sinkhole edged with frost. Somehow or other I managed to get hold of Howard's wrist and pull him out.

I remember little about Grandpa Larsen's death. Vague whisperings when he first got ill were soon replaced by Grandma's full blown shout, "Hvis du dør-da blir vi sittende fint i det" (If you die, won't <u>we</u> be in a fine fix!). She blamed Grandpa for his own demise as he wouldn't go to a doctor until it was too late. Grandpa had developed a sore on his lip that didn't heal, attributed to his pipe smoking. During the Great Depression and War Years he picked up discarded cigarette butts off the street, removed the tobacco for his ever-present pipe. The resultant cancer spread to his face. An April 1, 1943 operation was unsuccessful. Day remembers crying when she visited him in the hospital, "I got so scared when I saw the big white bandage that covered half his face." Grandpa died on July tenth of the same year.

I know we kids didn't go to his funeral. Howard and I were only eight, Day ten. My sister says she was sent to the movie, <u>Blood Behind the Sun</u>, with a neighbor friend. Howard and I were probably sent to Aunt Ethel's.

Uncle Gunnar and Aunt Frances came from Detroit, Michigan, and slept in Ma's big bed. I remember standing at the foot of that bed gaping at their small terrier snuggled between them. They adored dogs and treated them as if they were the children they never had. When Uncle Gunnar died in 1967 he was cremated, the urn with his ashes buried at the foot of one of their dog's graves in a pet cemetery in Detroit, Michigan.

I recall riding in Uncle Gunnar's coupe' with Ma, too, on an errand regarding Grandpa's funeral. My uncle was in a high state of agitation and had the car window rolled down; every chance he got, he screamed curses at the drivers who dared pass him. Confused, I edged closer to Ma. I could not imagine him the same cherished, clever and kind brother I had come to know from family stories.

I'm positive we all grieved for Grandpa and that he was continually remembered over coffee when Grandma and Ma reminisced about their glory days. Grandpa never had really been a constant in our lives, so we kids seldom wondered where he was. If after rushing home from school Ma or Grandma had been gone I would have been panic-struck, I'm sure. In my mind Grandpa wasn't ever missing. If I didn't see him I guessed he was in his room behind the closed door. When he vanished from view forever, as if vaporized by the wave of a magician's wand, his disappearance barely registered on my consciousness. Like most all the adult males in our lives who appeared and disappeared so quickly, I came to imagine them as wispy dandelion seeds destined to blow away with the first strong gust from an ill wind. Yet, for a long time I believed if she wanted to, Grandma could retrieve Grandpa with her, "Kom og spise!" (Come and eat!) command. But she never did and he never reappeared. His passing could only bring disaster to our little band, in any case.

Our years in the Kronlund House seemed to go on forever, but in reality they lasted less than three years. In 1990 I was reminded of that time, as I closed my eyes and imagined a safe place, as instructed by the facilitator in a *Journalizing For Self Discovery* class. Eight years later, at the University of Iowa Elderhostel writing program, that same exercise evoked the same result: The sun-room of the old Kronlund house blazed into my mind's eye, the warm glow of its security enveloping me as it always does when I return to it in reverie.

BEYOND THE LIMITS

We lived ten more months in the old Kronlund house after Grandpa's death and though our day-to-day activities continued as before, our last Christmas in that magical place finally brought the realization that Grandpa was gone and that our favorite holiday would be forever dulled by his absence. Like the Santa Claus fantasy Grandpa's image slowly ebbed, leaving a sense that somehow or other I had been cheated.

I attended Sunday School sporadically but never thought to turn to the church for succor. In my mind the ministers I had known up to that point in time were old, grim-faced Lutherans, the church itself ruled by a few stone-faced, ramrod-straight and stalwart families who would never share their power base with the less prosperous amongst them. Once, after Sunday school, as I passed a group of those first-families clustered on the steps, I overheard someone say, "She's a such a nice girl. It's a shame she can't get the adults in her family to come to church." It made tears well inside me and for a long time after, I tried as hard as I could to convince Ma to attend, but she resisted. She once said, "Don't pester me. I've had enough churching to last a lifetime. It's your turn, now." Her words left me with the idea that there was something naughty about me that only churchgoing could cure.

Our spinster teacher's continual repetition of children's bible stories, particularly Noah, Daniel and Jonah, did little but instill a sense of doom in me. For one thing, I suspected our family would have been washed away in the flood, since I had never heard or believed we were related in any way to Noah's clan. Just reading the words in "Daniel And The Lion's Den" filled me with terror. It was as if I could hear my bones crack as a limb was ripped from its socket by one of those hungry beasts. As for being swallowed by Jonah's whale, I was positive I'd never have been spat out; I would have been ground up in the cogs of the whale's digestive system.

I did enjoy participating in Easter and Christmas pageants and remember being in the children's choir for a short time. Those holiday celebrations seemed pleasant enough until my furtive glance fell on the statue of Jesus in the church nave and I felt a stabbing pain in my left hand. Matthew's words (25:41) exploded in my head: *Then he will say to those at his left hand, "Depart from me, you cursed, into the eternal fire prepared for the devil and his angels."*

Once Easter holidays ended I looked forward to release from my tie to the church, though its indelible stamp on me could not be erased. On May 29, 1944, when we moved to 6408 Oakes Avenue, just beyond the city limits, I came to believe that God had punished our little band by casting us out of our Eden into a world *"filled with hardship and sorrow,"* and, that due to my inability to inspire Ma or Grandma to return to the church, it was all my fault.

Our move was more likely precipitated by the loss of Grandpa's old-age pension. My sister reminds me that Ma was always behind in rent payments and utility bills, so perhaps we were evicted by our landlord, The Wisconsin State Bank.

The difference in the three-room hovel that we moved to on Sixty-fourth and Oakes and the Old Kronlund safe house, became more and more obvious to my nine-year-old eyes. Distinctly aware of the loss of Grandpa, I noticed the disappearance of all adult males, other relatives, and friends, and then the loss of decent housing and old possessions. Family rituals, meals together and entertaining disappeared as well. The worst loss in my mind was the loss of indoor plumbing. The dreaded outhouse was something I had only heard about from rural school friends and from stories Ma and Grandma told about Grandpa's brother old Pete Gilbertson's homestead.

I hated that toilet. Set in a ramshackle shed on the back lot, it was hot and rank. Hornets and wasps buzzed in its dark corners, flies wriggled in spider webs, their captors weaving the fine mesh ever tighter and tighter. I would clutch the rim of that bottomless black hole in terror that I'd fall in and at the same time, bang my dangling feet against its wood frame to frighten any larger creatures I imagined lurked below. Although I tried to follow Ma's advice, "Just get out there and do your business as fast as you can," it seemed an eternity before I could escape. Often while trapped on that hard, cold seat I wondered why God had felt compelled to create creepy things.

There were two floors in that rental property, the second uninhabitable due to a long ago fire. We all suffered fleeting headaches from the constant odor of charred wood and from the reeking fumes of Grandma's folk medicine cure for it, vinegar-soaked rags deposited across our foreheads. I came to associate all Grandma's health cures with torture. Oncoming colds would be abated with a fiery hot glass of lemonade that brought screams of, "It's burning my tongue!" Grandma showed no mercy. As the steamy brew coursed through our insides like flowing lava, she would bark, "Fort nå! Det er godt for deg!" (Fast now! It's good for you!). Her toothache cure was a hand-sewn square of flannel filled with salt and heated. I'm sure our screams echoed the neighborhood when that mini-pillow was pressed onto a cheek. The toothaches always disappeared, though I don't know if it was her medication or the scorching heat that shocked us into recovery. For gas on the stomach, Grandma would insist I lie on my belly across her footstool, while she thumped her fists on my lower back. Grandma always philosophized that, "Ondt Skal Ondt fordrive" (Bad can only be cured by bad). Other less dramatic cures were Listerine for mosquito bites and corn starch paste or butter for burns. There was no remedy for the pain that grew on my psyche though, bombarded as I was with daily reminders of our fall from grace.

Somehow or other eight rooms of furniture were shoved into three, with most smaller possessions left boxed or secured in the inescapable bundles and bags of newspapers for the duration of our tenancy. Ma deflected daily complaints from Grandma and us kids by assuring, "It's only temporary." I hoped against hope she was right, but like Grandma, I began to doubt that we would ever live well again.

Every available kitchen space was covered with dishes, clean and dirty. They were stacked on tables, boxes, the sink, and the unconnected gas stove. Meals consisted of sandwiches and canned soup, heated on an electric plate. Store-bought powdered-sugar donuts were constants. We ate standing up, or sitting on crates, or perched on the back stoop. Surprisingly, I was not too overwhelmed by my surroundings. I had become convinced that they were just punishment for my inability to be a better Christian, though I did at times feel a twinge of guilt seeing the rest of the family suffering for my sin.

A path between stacked furniture in the tiny living room led to the only completely clear space in the house, Grandma's windowed alcove housing the library table, lamp and her rocker. The brass bird cage and stand were in a corner of the space too, but the canary was gone. I dared not ask what happened to that bird, though suspected his disappearance was another curse inflicted by an unforgiving deity.

Grandma sat hour upon hour rocking, her tightly drawn mouth constantly moving like a cow chewing her cud. She mumbled in Norse, once shrieked aloud, "Dette er dråpen som får begeret til å flyte over" (This is the final straw!). Unable to get to her sewing machine or hand-sewing materials, she rocked away the endless days and nights. It was a particularly warm summer, so Grandma often used her Norse newspaper as a fan, the puffs of air from her movements generating waves of rubbing alcohol fumes. Though I didn't know it then, Grandma suffered from arthritis and splashed the rubbing-alcohol over her arms and hands daily for relief from constant aching muscles. Her long cotton dresses would be unbuttoned at the neck, eyes closed to the heat and clutter before her. I doubted if Grandma was even able to conjure up memories of her lost days of comfort and serenity in Larvik that she used to speak of, but no longer did.

The one minuscule bedroom with its bare ceiling light held three single-bed mattresses pushed side by side across the width of the floor. Naked, they held rumpled sheets in lieu of blankets, though most of the time it was too hot to use them. Ma's brass bed frame had disappeared along with Day's cast-iron crib. I suspect both were sold for scrap, hopefully melted down and put to good use for the war effort, as opposed to residing on display in an antique shop window. That end is easier to swallow and gives me comfort when those heirlooms pop into my mind. It seemed as if vestiges of the Larsen glory days vanished one by one with each of our moves, like a lost pilgrim's clothing dropped piece by piece as he stumbles to his death on vast, hot desert sands.

Ma and we three kids slept in that stuffy bedroom with its one sealed window, Grandma in her rocker, her stool and china pot near at hand. Pot emptying continued for us kids, though I never managed to get that burden all the way to the outhouse. About halfway there I'd stop and conceal myself behind a conveniently located honeysuckle bush. When the coast was clear I pitched the pot contents into the wasteland of our barren back yard. I suspected my siblings did the same, but with less guilt than that which consumed me.

We kids did manage a few small joys that summer. The moon-faced and skittish Wyman Rude trekked out to play with Howard, the only one of our friends to do so. There were no parties or company though, confirming my uneasy notion that we had been cast into a no-man's land. If we wanted to see other friends we'd start out early in the morning and return glutted at dusk, having stopped for sustenance at Aunt Ethel's in the old neighborhood.

Our new neighborhood was an especially fearful place due to two clans of raucous brothers, the Plasch and Sullivan boys, who seemed to lurk everywhere, like the creepy things I detested. Once when Howard, Wyman and I hiked past the nearby railroad tracks beyond a barbed wire fence to play war in the fields of wildflowers, bushes and trees that encircled our war zone, three of the Plasch boys came into view. Howard and Wyman dropped their wooden stick-rifles and sprinted ahead of me toward home. They'd gained a two-block edge when I tripped and fell. My screams didn't even slow them down. When one of the biggest of the Plasch bullies approached, I sprang to my feet, my rifle at the ready. As he turned his head to yell for his brothers, I walloped him across the stomach with that pseudo-rifle and took off running. I didn't look back until I reached the railroad tracks. The Plaschs were nowhere in sight. Loping home I found Howard and Wyman sitting on the porch crying, no doubt in terror at the thought of reporting my demise to the adults. I was thoroughly disgusted with both of them, though the exhilaration brought a faint inkling that the adventure put me back in favor with the powers that be. I envisioned myself Daniel, my foot straddling a dead lion, my rifle raised in defiance.

The only snapshot taken during our time beyond the city limits captures Day and me on the sagging front porch of our shanty. We're both in rumpled pajamas, our hair disheveled, barrettes askew, feet bare and grimy. I'm grinning ear-to-ear and hugging *Chi-Chi,* our rescued stray dog. Day looks utterly disheartened. She remembers nothing of that time, says she probably was reading. That could well be true. Ma often said, "I can't get that girl to do a thing. She's always got her nose in a book." Everyone but Grandma found ways to escape our hovel.

Howard and I spent a lot of time next door with the Lasfalk kids, tomboy Lu Lu Bell, and her pallid brothers, Walter and Fred, forever clothed in baggy, faded bib overalls. Their family kept chickens, geese, pigs and a cow. The backyard was a sea of mud and manure, with thick wooden planks traversing the area. With my arms akimbo for balance, I would extend my right foot and tap each plank until I located the steadiest one lower it, then carefully extend my left foot in front, inching along to the end like a circus trapeze artist. I often imagined myself a woeful seaman walking the plank in scenes from the popular pirate movies of the day, though instead of falling slow motion into the bounding main, I was sure I'd fall and be sucked into the muck beneath the wobbling plank.

One early morning, while everyone was still in bed, Howard and I crept outside to play catch. The ball I tossed to my twin went awry and landed in the Lasfalk yard; loping across to retrieve it, Howard attracted the attention of one of the largest of the Lasfalk geese. It charged my twin, in a flurry of squawking and flapping wings. Howard quickly shimmied up a nearby small tree, the goose circling below, his squawks rising in volume until, afraid they would wake everyone in the neighborhood, I hollered, "JUMP!" to my twin. He landed with a plop just beyond the planks, mud and muck spattering both of us. His survival was an amazement and relief to me, as I was always ready to cloak myself in guilt.

I was fascinated by the inside of the Lasfalk house. The doors between the rooms and the walls were covered with blankets and rugs, reminding me of scenes from Ma's favorite movie, *Desert Song.* Moving from room to room was like moving through a cool and dark tent, bringing to my mind the desert bazaar scene on Uncle Gunnar's Belgian tapestry. The Lasfalk kids had an impressive collection of comic books that we loved to pore over in their dim-lit living-room: *Blondie, Bomba the Jungle Boy, Elmer Fudd, Felix the Cat, Dick Tracy, Dumbo, Casper the Ghost, and Catwoman,* among others. My favorites were *Brenda Starr and Life with Archie.*

One joyful event was Howard and Lu Lu Bell's date to a Saturday matinee. It was the only time I saw Lu Lu Bell in a dress. Brilliant pink satin, trimmed with lace, I was sure it was her Sunday-best frock. Howard wore long pants and a shirt, his cowlick plastered down with hair tonic. I teased them both mercilessly, and, when they were led in for her inspection, Grandma chuckled and muttered, "Herre Gud!" (Holy God!).

Howard was later befriended by Adeline Nordeen, a massive, dark-haired woman who lived in an impressive house on our block and owned Elsie's Cafe on the east side of Tower Avenue between Fifty-eighth and Fifty-ninth Streets. She had a car and Howard often joined her on daily trips to the cafe. I think he did odd jobs there. Ma became concerned that he spent too much time with Adeline. My mother's uneasiness brought to my mind the story of Samson and Delilah, with the resultant silent prayer from me that our hovel would crash to the ground like the Philistine temple. I doubted there was anything sinister about Howard's new-found friendship; Adeline was just too old as far as I could see. Most adults over the age of twenty were old in my eyes. Ma seemed touched by jealousy and concern for us kids when we strayed too far afield.

Ma strayed far afield more often than ever, too. Besides her endless club meetings, she began visiting Grandma's old friends, with me in tow. In retrospect I suspect it was a diversion, a devious scheme to keep Grandma's prying cohorts from visiting us. It smacked of Grandma's touch, in any case. Often, wherever we lived, when she espied a neighbor or friend coming up the street toward our house, Grandma would shout to us to pull down the shades and lock the doors. She never appreciated uninvited guests, feeling it was a terrible breach of etiquette.

I loved our jaunts up Tower Avenue from Sixty-Fourth to Fifty-fifth Street to Mrs. Fregard or our bus trips downtown to Mrs. Burke, Mrs. Peterson or Mrs. Wick. I remember them as one, with their aura of warmth, their plump bodies and their gray hair, except for Ragna Burke, who had ink black hair, which, Ma once confided, was dyed. Those intrepid Norse ladies served delicious open-faced sandwiches and homemade pastries, so much missed by me after our move.

Grandma continued to follow daily war reports, constantly fretting over the state of the Norwegian people. She and Ma dug out our outgrown clothes, repacked them in a box and somehow or other scraped money together for postage. I wrote a note and inserted it in the pocket of my discarded beaver coat. The package was sent to Grandma's cousins' family in Larvik. I was thrilled to receive a thank-you note and picture of my fourth cousin Brit and her doll, the doll so large and lifelike I thought it was a baby sister. I couldn't help but notice that Brit's clothes, house and surroundings looked far better than ours, though I was grateful for the chance to make a bright red check on the plus column of my invisible list of good versus bad deeds.

In the 1940s pen pals were a popular pastime for grade schoolers. Besides my new found fourth cousin in Norway, I corresponded with a twelve year old boy in Lagos, Nigeria. That correspondence was destined to come to a halt after he wrote and asked for a radio. Ma helped me compose a response that she assured would cut him off, "before anything more got out of hand." I asked him for a tiger skin. He never wrote again and I never felt an ounce of guilt from that loss.

Our old cathedral-style table radio continued blasting the day-to-day war news, Grandma's need to keep abreast of world events never wavering. On June 6 it was full of news that D-Day had begun. Ma said, "I'll bet that's why we haven't heard from Damer lately," but we seldom heard from my father, anyway. World War II Victory mail, letters written on government-issued stationary, were photographed, the film then shipped overseas for development and the pictures sent out as letters. My sister remembers one that our father sent while in Florida training, wherein he mentioned all the "cute little pickaninies." That phrase rankles my sister still. Only one of my father's three communiqués' survives: *"Dear folks: Just got your present and thanks very much. I guess you know that I am now in France and its pretty much like every other country except that it's nearly Christmas and its still nice and green here. It hasn't snowed any but it sure has rained plenty and it's plenty muddy. We live in tents and they have stoves in them so we aren't so bad off as some of the boys over here. I have been to Paris and seen the Arch of Triumph and the unknown soldier grave which is right under the arch. We also saw Napoleon's Tomb and the Eiffel Tower and we went through the Cathedral of Notre Dame all of which were very interesting. We saw a lot of other places too numerous to mention. It was a kind of tour with a guide to tell us all about each place. I only have one kick tho' cause it rained all day and I couldn't do much shopping, also there ain't much to buy. I guess that's all I can think of now except to thank all of you for the present 'cause I really enjoyed it. Damer."*

Years later I learned that prior to the invasion, like all combat servicemen, our father was required to make out a will. He arranged for his demise by naming his sister Millie, his Army Air Force life insurance beneficiary. As Aunt Rose's 1990s care giver, I recall the hollow anguish I felt reading that entry aloud to her while struggling to keep my voice from breaking. Though that pain persists in me, a story my sister related might account for my father's seemingly cruel action.

Back in Superior in 1967 from New Haven, Connecticut, my sister took her four young children to meet their grandfather. While relating World War II stories, Damer told my sister that our mother had turned him in to the Draft Board. Confronted with that accusation, our mother vehemently denied it, but went on to tell my sister that at the time our father was unemployed and not supporting his kids, yet using us as excuses to avoid military service.

After my return to Superior in May 1990, I met a friend of his, who on learning that Damer was my father said, "I never knew he had a family." I retorted, "That's the impression he wanted to give." The only time our father acknowledged us was in the copy of his will I received after his death in June 1990. It stated, "It is my intent to leave nothing to my children." His entire estate went to his special friend of fifty years.

One day in July, the radio blared an exciting report: *"A*

bomb was thrown at Hitler yesterday, but he was only slightly injured." More mundane disasters were skirting our lives at Sixty-Fourth Street and Oakes Avenue.

One evening just after Grandma pushed herself up out of her rocker and hobbled on her cane along the box-lined path to the kitchen, the ceiling fell. Chunks of lath, plaster and mortar landed in a cloud of dust on her vacated rocker. Grandma's "Herra Guds!" reverberated through the open alcove windows onto the night air. I was sure it was my fault, recalling my wish that the whole house collapse. After that disaster Ma intensified her efforts to locate a decent house. Through her friend, Jennie Wright, a family Jennie was acquainted with offered the front apartment in their hulking duplex at 5927 Oakes Avenue, back in the city limits. I clapped in glee at Grandma's, "Takk til gud fra morgen til kveld!" (Thanks to God from morning to night!). I was ecstatic at the prospect of being reunited with Lois Paul and other grade school friends. The only prayer of gratefulness I knew popped into my head: "Thank you for the food we eat, thank you for the world so sweet, thank you God for EVERY-thing!" It had suddenly occurred to me that our three-month sojourn beyond the city limits was the exact same amount of time spent by Moses and the children of Israel after escaping from the Egyptians and finding Mt. Sinai. My siblings and I had narrowly escaped the looming prospect of attending Billings School that autumn, as required by all children living beyond the city limits. We would return to Wm. Cullen Bryant Grade School, my Mt. Sinai.

WILLIAM CULLEN BRYANT
GRADE SCHOOL
(1940-1949)

I think I remember the names of early teachers because they all made an impact on who I became. Then too, Ma was active in the PTA. She regularly commented, "You'll like her, she's such a nice person," about one or another of them, including principal, Miss Ballou, my mother's favorite and one of her first teachers. *"Of course Miss Ballou catered to me,"* Ma once said. "She'd had Gunnar in her class first and when she found out he was my brother, I could do no wrong," quickly adding, "...not that I would!"

I thought the name was Blue and a dumb name at that, doubly so when attached to the hated appellation, Ethel. Miss Ballou, ancient in my eyes, confirmed this by the fact of her retirement during the second half of our Kindergarten term. She was replaced by Mr. Taylor, whom I don't remember at all, and then, Mr. Bowles, whose tenure lasted through the rest of my grade school years. I remember Mr. Bowles' thick head of wavy white hair and his lantern jaw. I thought him quite handsome.

I thought my first four teachers had lovely names: Miss Rockwell, Miss Henretty (Kindergarten), Miss Underhill (Grade One) and Miss Sweetnum (Grades Two and Three). My fondness for those names doubled after learning their first names of Fern, Mary Jo, Violet and Ina, respectively. It must have been during the time I began collecting names, at Aunt Ethel's urging, "You should have a hobby, so you won't be so bored while you're here." It was no doubt an attempt on Auntie's part to deflect my curiosity during her Sunday gossip sessions with Ma and Grandma Oliphant. I was never bored, sitting still, hands folded, eyes closed, all the while silently testing my memory by tracing the thread of their long, drawn-out tales of local scandal and corruption backwards, to their source.

Ever anxious to please, I took up Aunt Ethel's challenge.

90

I think that my constant pestering for assistance annoyed the women at times, though. Vexed, Grandma Oliphant once complained, "You really started something now, Ethel," though all three women were quick to help me along. Ma's contributions included ancient Norse names like Hansena, Serena, and Simonia. Grandma Oliphant's offerings were more poetical: Charity, Faith, Grace, and Hope. Once started, Grandma would wander off onto her favorite subject of Scot's historical figures, continuously recounting, "You're descended from Sir Walter Oliphant who married Elizabeth, daughter of Robert Bruce." Ma would counter, "Don't forget your Norwegian blood. We are descended from the Vikings and invaded Scotland long before Robert Bruce was around." Aunt Ethel would intervene and remind the women of the subject at hand. Ever practical, she contributed favorite names of the day, Judy, Patsy, Peggy and Polly. She liked Mary best, said for a simple name it had a lofty meaning in Gaelic: exalted.

Though Miss Mary Steuber may well have qualified as being exalted, her fourth grade class was agony to me. She bestowed upon me the honor of putting her kettle on for tea next door in the teacher's lounge at exactly five minutes before noon. The problem was, I couldn't tell time. I often feigned deep preoccupation, head down, nose in a text book. At zero hour Miss Steuber never failed to tap her sharp lead pencil on her desk and tilt her head like a robin listening for earthworms. Peering over her Grannie glasses, she would look at the clock and say, "Frances? Time." Quite diminutive except for a prominent nose, Miss Steuber brought to mind *The Witch of the West*. She had a distinctive walk that gave a false notion of delicacy. Listing to the right with shoulder in the lead, Miss Steuber sauntered around the classroom with her hand daintily upturned, much like movie star Bette Davis, sans the cigarette.

As a fifth grader in Miss (Alice) Anderson's class, I got lots of attention with my story telling. Fantasies about lost cats, dogs and children were my forte.' The adventures were replete with lonely country roads, spooky cemeteries, haunted Victorian houses and narrow escapes, peppered with lots of "...and then they...," followed by yet another entanglement. The sagas often ended a bit abruptly as I seldom knew where they were going when I set out. The unraveling took most all the class time allotted for that activity and my classmates, knowing my bent for long-windedness, urged me on. If they were called on first they insisted, "Let Frances talk," anxious to get off the hook. Everyone seemed content with the situation except my twin. During my presentations Howard lowered his head onto his crossed arms and pretended to sleep, emitting false snoring sounds that brought a ripple of giggles across the room. The harshest reprimand uttered by the soft in body and heart Miss Anderson was, "Hush now children." At other times my twin tried to distract me by crossing his eyes, pulling his mouth sideways and sticking his tongue out. Miss Anderson never scolded him as they were fast friends. Howard recalled that she once bought him a blue plastic flute.

My twin and other grade five peers had better singing voices than me, though. My gift was fervor, not harmony. Mr. Bowles once stopped in as Miss Anderson blew a thin metallic note on her pitch pipe and we stood to sing The National Anthem. I crowed and preened, mouthing the parts I couldn't carry, aware that a freight train thundering past on the nearby railroad tracks drowned our voices. After the performance Mr. Bowles said, "That little girl in the back row sure is enthusiastic. Maybe she could give us a solo." I heard the titters of my classmates and felt heat rise on my neck. Mumbling through my off-key rendition, my wavering gaze fixed on the principal's crotch. Mr. Bowles was staring blankly into space while nervously pulling the zipper on his pants up and down in time to the beat of Miss Anderson's accompaniment. Solo singing ended for me that day. By sixth grade, when called back to demonstrate the art of story-telling to new fifth grade students, I had seemingly lost that talent, as well. Miss Anderson never invited me again.

I blossomed as a sixth grader in Mrs. Osmundson's combined fifth and sixth grade class. Ma said she and Mrs.
Osmundson's in-laws, "..went as far back as our 1903 immigration to Superior," and that, "As a teen, I baby-sat Mrs.
Osmundson's brother-in-law, Clarence." Whenever we ran into
him on downtown window-shopping trips and stopped to chat,
Ma would say to him, "Can you believe that I used to hold you
on my lap?" Her words brought an uneasy disquiet in me, he
being a grown man by then.

Mrs. Osmundson's reading hour was a favorite. She
enthralled us with her rendition of a chapter a day from *The
Secret Garden.* She was taken sick during that time, Lois Paul,
Doris Raulerson and I were elected to deliver a gift to her from
our two classes. We felt honored to be welcomed into a teacher's
inner sanctum, equating it with being guests at the White House.

Mrs. Johnson substituted during Mrs. Osmundson's absence. Her husband Douglas taught General Science and Physical Education at Bryant. I was quite taken aback by that information. It was hard for me to imagine such an ordinary, un-
adorned woman tied to the handsome, athletic "Doug," as he
was referred to by Bryant boys' sports-team members. I hated
the flat drone of Mrs. Johnson's speaking voice and convinced
myself that it was the reason I could not remember the conclu-
sion of *The Secret Garden,* when I tried to write the required
book report.

During the second half of sixth grade, I was promoted
to Miss (Helen) McKone's *"A"* section, together with Doris
Raulerson, who by then was flaunting her intellectual compe-
tence to the point of nausea amongst our less endowed peers. In
an effort to steel myself against her superiority complex, I resolved to be kind, charitable and fun-loving amongst those same
peers, ever mindful of Grandma Larsen's repetitious maxim,
"Som man reder, så ligger man" (As you sow, so shall you reap).
That never worked with my twin.

Left behind in Mrs. Osmundson's "B" group, Howard

took to chanting, "Brown nose, brown nose!" whenever he learned of any small triumph on my part. The silent eye we had always kept out for each other seemed to be fast waning. My twin's mocking stirred a queasy, helpless feeling in me, sensing as I did that any little success on my part could only reflect failure on his. When my twin got into a playground fight with Robert Mittlestadt, Howard was knocked to the ground and punched in the face. The resultant bloody nose brought him to tears. I did nothing to comfort my twin, only feeling a strange grief replace my usual helplessness, and I guiltily concluded that my brother was a weakling. There could perhaps have been a more pedestrian reason for my apparent callousness, though. The clue lies in a long-ago diary. After several blank pages this one-line entry appears: *" I love school!"* The next day's two-line clarification, reads: *"A new boy is in my class. His name is Robert Middlestadt."*

In spite of her somber bearing I liked Miss McKone well enough. Her bony face, high cheekbones and sunken eye sockets gave the appearance of a tightly-stretched rubber mask. My initial feeling of inadequacy in that sixth grade classroom had nothing to do with Miss McKone. It lay with what I conceived to be my brainier and higher-stationed peers. Except for my nemesis, Doris Raulerson and for the pale, bright-eyed, Donald Keith Larson, the class was filled with students who lived on the east side of Tower Avenue. I thought that side of Superior's main street a better neighborhood than ours. Among the A group were two prim females, Joanne Gunderson and Diane Peterson. There were popular basketball players: tall and loose limbed, Lester Hagman, platinum-haired Adonis, Jim Hulter, squeaky-clean, Donald Nummi and compact, wiry, Bucky Johnson, residing there as well. My twin once revealed to me that Lester and Bucky teased him mercilessly. Howard's disclosure brought mixed emotions, because at one time I had crushes on both boys. Bucky was short, with olive skin and the palest of blue eyes. Once as the noonday buzzer erupted and everyone rushed for the exits, his elbow brushed against my chest, sending me into a tailspin of ecstasy.

My twin said, "I eventually got my revenge on Bucky." One winter evening Howard encountered his nemesis behind the ice rink warming shed. Alone, Bucky attempted a phony smile of good will, and in a shaky voice said, "Hi Howie, how ya doin'?" Without a word Howard pulled off an ice-caked mitten and slapped it across Bucky's face.

I hated recess. My friends Lois, Doris and Donna were adept on the jungle-gym, often somersaulting over the highest bar. Fear of pain kept me from that activity, having had seen the wounds and heard the screams of classmates after tumbles on the cinder-coated playground expanse. I was content to glide back and forth on the swings with the younger kids. I hated baseball, too, especially after I'd stood frozen in horror on seeing the dark-eyed, flamboyant Bertha Zuber knocked cold by an errant rock-hard baseball. Positioning myself far outfield, I hoped against hope that no one would hit a fly. If a ball did spiral toward me I'd cover my face with my arms and duck.

Though we were required to take Physical Education, I did not do well. Luckily Miss (Ida) Doleysh always gave me a passing grade. I remember little of Miss Doleysh's gym classes except for the silver whistle on a black gross-grain ribbon that hung around her neck. Everything else about her seemed archaic, especially her near ankle-length print dresses, wool knit shawls and black laced oxfords, identical to Grandma Larsen's garb.

Although physical activity was abhorrent I shined when it came to the continuing day to day pursuit of my grade-school education. By seventh grade I was at the top of my class with Bonnie Andrews, an effervescent, talented artist, Inez Lisdahl, a tall, modest, popular girl; and my cohorts, Doris Raulerson, Donna Sands and Mary Ann Schneeberger, among others. The brilliant Mary Ann came late to Bryant and had a near-hysterical, high-pitched and spontaneous laugh. She was a blue-baby according to Ma and because my mother always encouraged me to, "Be kind to the weak and downtrodden," I took Mary Ann into my fold.

Seventh and eighth grades brought some self-confidence as I flourished under the charge of teachers Miss (Ella) Biggs, Miss (Ida) Dolyesh, Miss (Florence) Gustafson, Miss (Helen) Ivey, Miss (Helen) McKone and Mr. (Douglas) Johnson. They taught Social Science, English, Music, Math, Art and General Science respectively.

I didn't do at all well in Home Economics with Mrs. (Helen) Skoog, however. All my Cream of Wheat and oatmeal attempts burnt and the rickrack on the apron we were required to complete was always ripped out by the "Black Beetle," as Mrs. Skoog came to be known. Tall and solid, her graying hair was stacked in a bun on top of her head. She wore a perpetual frown on her pasty face, bringing to mind a prison matron. At Doris Raulerson's urging I stole a banana and hid it in the cloakroom. Mrs. Skoog was incensed, demanded an immediate confession from the unknown culprit. Everyone remained silent. As punishment we were all kept in the school kitchen through lunch. Mrs. Skoog, ranting a lecture on honesty, became so inflamed that she forgot she was due at a Central High afternoon class until Mr. Bowles popped into the room to remind her. Doris and I never divulged that sin to our peers.

Miss Biggs was just over five feet tall, wispy-looking with infinite spiderweb wrinkles and laugh lines crisscrossing her crimped face. A plethora of carefully waved gray hair from her brow to the nape of her neck terminated in a braided knot, the entire creation encased in a hair net. Miss Biggs' myopic blue eyes behind wire-rimmed glasses, were bright and lively. When annoyed with her, I'd punctuate my complaints to my peers with, "That beady-eyed old maid." I had no idea that in those years female teachers in our school district could not marry. The exception was Mrs. Osmundson, whom I suspect was originally from another state. Once, referring to my teacher and her

96

in-laws, Ma said, "But then the Osmundson's realize Minnie's not a Superior girl."

Oddly to me, Mrs. Skoog was an exception, too. The subliminal message I got from that knowledge was that only married women could be capable cooks and seamstresses. Though often gaga over one or another of my male peers, marriage was never a priority. In another long ago diary entry I wrote: *"My childhood ambitions are: 1. Dancer. 2. Congresswoman. 3. Kindergarten Teacher. 4. Gym Teacher. 5. Housewife."*

Besides being our Social Studies teacher, Miss Biggs was the stamp club advisor; I was the president of that club. My favored position put me in the spotlight with her, though I soon learned it was a position of risk. I made the mistake of pasting all the canceled stamps I'd accumulated into my five and dime stamp-book. Miss Biggs howled with laughter, informed me that the correct procedure was to use special tape that allowed the stamps to be removed and rearranged. That ego deflating episode was doubly galling, as I had hoped to win top prize for my creation. Instead little Bobby Fudally, a giggly baby-faced boy two years my junior, won first prize for his blocked and framed collection of old, rare stamps his grandfather had given him. For a long time after I referred to Bobby as, "That puny little snot." Miss Biggs' derision was a source of particular agony as my fellow club-members were present at my dressing-down. I felt especially betrayed by secretary Mary Ann Schneeberger's grating laughter and felt she owed me some loyalty seeing as how I had so charitably taken her under my wing. Miss Biggs' popularity substantially diminished in my mind after that incident. The only saving grace was her fondness for my twin.

Once during a classroom discussion of monetary issues Miss Biggs asked for a definition of money. Howard waved his hand wildly and when called on said, "Money is the root of all evil!" Miss Biggs hooted in appreciation. Years later I learned that my cousins, first Jim and then Pat Mockler, were favorites of hers when she taught at Howe School in the 1930s. I can only conclude that Miss Biggs had an affinity for rambunctious, if not disruptive boys. Howard personified that ilk. Once my twin broke into the eighth grade girl's locker room, put a nickel in the Kotex machine and waved the pad over his head and chased me and my classmates through the gymnasium. Never mind that few of us knew what purpose the fluffy napkin served. Howard was severely reprimanded by Mr. Bowles for that prank.

I was surprised to learn that my sister was fond of Miss Biggs. One day, after Marvin Wells' on-going harassment, Day was moved to tears and ran into the girl's cloakroom. Miss Biggs was there adjusting her cotton slip, asked my sister, "What's wrong with you?" Day blurted, "Marvin keeps trying to grab me and kiss me, or pull up my skirt." He never bothered Day again. We've concluded that our teacher spoke to Marvin's folks. Even I can't imagine that scene though I knew when rankled, Miss Biggs could strike fear in the hearts of us students. It would have been astounding at that point in time for me to know she could browbeat adults, as well.

Although I could not tolerate Miss Doleysh's gym classes, I did well in her English class and always received *A's* in both seventh and eighth grade. I remember coveting a lapel locket she wore. It was gold and hung from a delicate filigreed bow. I imagined it held a picture of a long lost World War One love, perhaps because of the jaunty dark berets she had an infinity for. From the stories Ma told me of Uncle Gunnar's service I knew most yanks in that conflict had served in France.

Miss Gustafson was a peacock among the female sparrows of our grade school teachers. Younger than our other mentors, she was tall and flamboyant. When she neared my desk a mist of cloying perfume descended like a gossamer veil. Her natural curly mane of shoulder-length strawberry blond hair brought on-going debates by us girls of, "Does she or doesn't she dye?" At times Miss Gustafson's makeup seemed applied with a spatula. She favored bronze foundations, bright orange lipsticks and heavily drawn auburn eyebrow pencil. From the distance of my back row desk and shortsighted gaze, Miss Gustafson appeared a blob of orange. She was perhaps attempting to cover the masses of brown freckles on her thin, lantern-jawed face. It never worked. Her neck and her pale arms, exposed beneath capped sleeves, were blanketed with those dreaded blotches. In the 1940s ivory satin, clear skin was the goal of most females, personified by teenage movie star Elizabeth Taylor.

Miss Gustafson's dresses skirted her knees. They were brightly hued, low-cut for that era, and tight, due to a tendency toward plumpness. My twin and the other boys in her classes all had crushes on her. I tittered aloud when Doris insisted Miss Gustafson's mascara clotted eyelashes batted in Mr. Bowles' or Mr. Johnson's presence. It's no wonder that whenever she got overly pudgy, wild unsubstantiated rumors circulated that Miss Gustafson was pregnant. We were especially excited with that idea after long weekends or school holidays when she returned looking slim and trim. We then decided that she had had an abortion. Our salacious interest in Miss Gustafson's sex life was no doubt partially tinged with envy at the attention she generated.

Miss Ivey was perfect in my eyes. She wore fashionable dresses with matched princess collars secured with natty short silk scarves, patent leather belts and low-heeled pumps. Her gathered-at-the-waist dress skirts reached just below her knees and gently wafted when she walked. Their patterns tended to be muted geometrical forms on gray or beige backgrounds with perfectly matched button earrings. Ma said that Miss Ivey probably bought her clothes at Lightbody's or Roth Brothers Department store. That knowledge was the basis of a long-lasting, favorite daydream of mine. Hidden in Roth Brothers until closing, I would saunter from area to area gathering perfectly matched ensembles and accessories and carefully fold them into the distinctive logoed Roth Brothers suit boxes. The puzzle of how that escapade would end was never a part of my daydream, though I did look for hiding places whenever in that store with Ma.

Miss Ivey was of medium height, her jet black hair parted in the middle and softly fluffed just below her ears. Though she wore coke-bottle thick tortoiseshell glasses, they magnified strong and kind eyes. Miss Ivey's subject of Math was not a favorite of mine, but she taught it with gentle understanding. I always sensed that when our teachers voted between Doris Raulerson and me for the coveted American Legion Leadership Award, I got her vote. She once told me, "Personality is sometimes more important than intelligence." It pains me to recall that it was her desk that Doris and I rifled looking for math exam results.

My mother knew that Miss Ivey took care of her elderly father in their family home at 2320 Tower Avenue. She always pointed out the house when we passed on our bus trips downtown. That house draws my eye still. In 1997 I read a feature article in the local newspaper about a Mrs. Ivey who was celebrating her one hundredth birthday. In the picture sitting next to her was her sister-in-law and care giver, Helen Ivey. I was amazed that she was still in that family home. Miss Ivey passed away a year later at age ninety-seven.

I was reunited with Miss McKone in seventh grade and gained a special respect for her artistic talents. She often praised the work I did in my favorite medium of finger painting. All those creations tended to be clumped in reds, oranges and purples. My other creations, whether in chalk, pencil or watercolor, were of small white cottages surrounded with flower gardens, trees and a white picket fence.

I remember Mr. Johnson as a charmer. His General Science class was a treat, especially when I would be hunkered over the microscope and he hovered nearby. He exuded a musky, mingled with body odor, aura. Though he was slightly bald and wore glasses, he had a beautiful smile heightened by deep dimples. We girls thought him quite handsome and interesting, as he was extremely dedicated to his subject. Muscular and tanned, he no doubt worked out as his second subject was Physical Education. I remember crowding around the edges of the basketball court gym with my giggling girlfriends, trying to get a glimpse of him in his sleeveless tee shirt and shorts. Wishful fantasizing had me hoping Mr. Johnson had a roving eye and that it would someday fall on me.

In the early 1990s when my sister and I were having a yard sale, she pointed out an elderly couple and said it was Mr. and Mrs. Douglas Johnson. The only thing I recognized about him were his dimples. I didn't reveal my identity to either of them, now realize it was a defining moment. Me and the people around me were fast aging. In grade school I thought I would never get old and that those near and dear to me would never change. By the fall of 1944 my beloved grandma had already changed, though it would be years before I recognized that fact.

A CALL TO ARMS

Grandma's near disaster, after escaping death by falling mortar at Sixty-Fourth and Oakes, seemed a call to arms for her. Once settled in the Hellesen duplex, she threw herself back into command and assumed a fiery presence more pronounced than ever. Though respect and deference was still expected, Grandma's hostility exploded unchecked, small irritations splat like dropped eggs and the constant drip of resentment eroded any armor of constraint she may still have possessed. It was as if Grandma came to realize there was no point in brooding, that things were not going to get better, that she was where she was destined to be. I can almost hear her defiant voice, "Gjørt er gjørt!" (What's done is done! There is no more!).

That turn of events is easy for me to understand now. The houses of my youthful remembrances could only have compounded the day to day bombardment of real and imagined insults, to Grandma.

Fairfax Hall was one of the sites of her housekeeper degradation, brought on when the last of her inheritance monies evaporated from the support of two families their first year in America, her own and old Pete Gilbertsen's brood. Once Uncle Gunnar learned to speak English, Grandma set off with him in tow to rent a house. She and Grandpa went to work, as a housemaid and factory worker, respectively, in stark contrast to their days of middle-class leisure in Norway. And though they managed to reestablish that status and provide Ma and Gunnar with all the comforts of their station, my grandparents worked long and hard. Worst of all, they never were able to own a home of their own in America.

During Ma's young adulthood and Grandma's matronly years, the Old Kronlund House was one of the centers of their social life. The Kronlund family included the Larsens on guest lists for parties, numerous trips to their Eau Claire Lakes summer home and special family and Bethel Church functions. The country trips in the Kronlund's Model T Ford, bouncing over rutted backwoods roads, often brought Grandma's shrieks of "Herre Gud!," a remembrance learned from Kronlund daughter, Ethel Kronlund Nelson. The Kronlund's could not have known that Grandma's outbursts were compounded by her ever festering hostility. Whenever she spoke of Mr. Kronlund Grandma referred to him as, "..nothing but a saloon-keeper." The old Kronlund house must have brought severe irritation to Grandma's psyche during those three years of occupancy with us grand kids.

The Sixty-Fourth Street house, the most abominable memory prompter of all, had a horrific similarity to the Larsen's first land of opportunity residency just blocks away from our shack. That first dwelling was a three-room hovel with an outhouse in back, as well. I can not imagine how it housed four adults and six children.

We were now settled in the Hellesen duplex. One lot north stood a house Grandma and Grandpa attempted to purchase during the Depression, but could not scrape together the twenty-five dollar price tag. One block south, moved from its original site on Central Avenue, stood the house where Grandma suffered the loss of her stillborn son.

Grandma's seeming histrionics over having her nose rubbed in gall toward the end of her life had one favorable effect as far as we kids were concerned. She no longer objected to more than one pet at a time in the house. Stray dogs attached themselves to one or the other of us kids and were welcomed into the fold. Chi-Chi was the first, then Boy, Buster and Kawlija. All came and went over time and except for Kawlija, were mature dogs. Kawlija was received as a puppy and fated to be our companion into the 1950s.

Cats sauntered unrestrained through our time in the Hellesen duplex. Most were offspring of the forever pregnant Pansy, named for Ma's favorite flower. Grandma seemed always to know when Pansy was ready to deliver. A cardboard box, filled with clean rags would appear behind the front room heater and in a day or two Pansy strolled into the room, sniffed and pressed the material and then curved herself into the center of the box to doze. As soon as Pansy exhibited discomfort by kneading the rags and softly mewing, Grandma shooed us kids out of the room. We could hear her cooing and encouraging Pansy through the process, but had no clue as to what was going on. Once, home from grade school for lunch, Grandma wasn't in the kitchen. We three rushed to the living room in time to see her gently pull out the last of the litter. I was dumbfounded to notice that the slimy, squirming newborn seemed to have been extracted from Pansy's bottom. We pushed closer to Grandma, only to have her shriek her mad-with-power Marine Sergeant command, "UT! UT! Nå!!" (Out! Out, now!). By our return after school there was only one kitten left.

As soon as Pansy left the birthing box, Grandma would banish her from the house, fill our round steel bathtub with warm water, lower a sack of mewing kittens and then cover the bag with an inverted pail weighted down with a brick. Each bundle, carefully wrapped in a torn sheet, was buried under the lilac bushes outside. We came to accept Grandma's kitten executions. She decreed early on that we could only keep one kitten from each litter. Still, we ended up with plenty of Pansy's offspring to love. Of them, I remember Fuzzy Wuzzy, Lucky, Panther, Pumpkin, Salt, and Pepper, and Toughy Tiger.

Grandma's epiphany brought with it a surge of furious energy. She insisted on keeping the three first floor rooms neat and orderly. I came to associate those rooms as Grandma's domain up until her death in 1948. A constant there, she was busily back to her household chores. Grandma's huge rocker, positioned in front of the parlor window next to the library table, once again gave her a clear view to the bus stop, two blocks east down Sixtieth Street. At her post one late evening, lights out, drapes open, Grandma noticed a man lurking behind a tree on the nearby corner. She rose from her chair and pulled the drapes across her face, leaving a crack open to continue her surveillance. The man came across the lawn up to the window. As he shaded his eyes and pressed against the windowpane, Grandma threw open the drapes and shouted, "Hva skal du HA!!! (What do you WANT!?) It was said that the man's hat fell to the ground as he took off running, never to be seen in the neighborhood again.

Grandma took up her rag-rug and sewing projects, though her rocking motions now seemed faster and more pronounced. Even Grandma's trek through the dining-bedroom area to the kitchen was notable. She thumped her cane on the carpetless floors as if crushing hard-crusted beetles. If in her line of passage, we kids would bolt out of her path. That first fall Grandma tacked felt insulation strips around all the windows on the first floor and hung old blankets over the hallway and back doors, determined we would be snug and warm when winter descended.

Grandma resumed her cooking duties as well, though often she shrieked for assistance as the kitchen setup was not to her liking. For one thing the two burner gas stove and small oven weren't conducive to bygone Kronlund House creations. She had to reduce former grandiose menus to pots of soup, boiled potatoes, lots of fried fish and the forever recurrent Spanish Delight hot dish. We knew when Grandma's explosions were imminent, as she would bang the cast iron frying pan onto the gas stove grill and crash pots and pans against the cracked enamel sink, where only one of the two taps worked, and that only supplying cold water.

Our new digs in the Hellesen duplex were just one cut above the old, though there was indoor plumbing, such as it was. The toilet worked but the bathtub was not connected and there was no hot water upstairs either. My youthful fear of closed doors returned, compounded by the fact that the toilet was on the second floor above a wainscoted and doored enclosure, halfway up the hallway stairs. There were two doors in the down-stairs hallway, as well, one off the living room and one off the kitchen. Both were kept closed to conserve any heat that ema-nated from the front and dining room coal stoves. The door to the kitchen could not have been opened anyway, as Ma's boxes of newspapers and magazines, stacked to the ceiling at the deeper end of the hall, blockaded any hope of access.

A new sofa bed appeared as if by magic in the front room. It was opened at night for Ma and one or another of us kids to sleep on. I hated its hardness and giant seam in the middle. I was forever sliding into that uncomfortable crevice. Ma's pi-ano and music stand were in the front room, too. Only one other rocker fit there. The rest were relegated to storage upstairs amongst the flotsam and jetsam of other old furniture and relics in their last stages of decrepitude. There were three windows, two facing east and one facing south. The cherished library table fronted the south window.

The two windows in the dining room faced south, also. Ma's vanity stood in a corner next to one of the windows, a mission oak and leather day bed, left by a former tenant, occu-pied the opposite corner of the south wall. The dining room table was centered in the middle of the room, the side board and a single bed with a coal heater at its head, were on either side of the table, against opposite walls. It was a strange setup in my eyes. I had never seen beds in the dining rooms of my friends' houses and certainly not a piss-pot. That abomination once again occupied its throne at the foot of Grandma's bed, though it was concealed beneath the bed during the day. Pot dumping became an especially detestable task as we had to carefully mince through the hallway and up the stairs hugging that heavy relic close to our chests while praying its acrid contents wouldn't spill.

The kitchen had a wobbly wood table that we tried to keep clear as ordered by Grandma, but failed on occasion. Once when Ma was away to a Daughters of Norway convention, we kids, in a state of unusual mutiny, refused to wash dishes. By week's end there was not one clean dish left in the house. The crusted china soon overflowed the table, sink, stove and all other free spaces. As we frolicked outside with our neighborhood friends the night Ma was destined to return, Grandma stomped out onto the front porch, waved her cane in the air and demanded our instant presence in the kitchen.

Humiliated in front of our cohorts, one or the other of us sassed her, prompting Grandma's forever, "HOLD KJEFT!" (SHUT UP!) command. We sheepishly filed into the house where we spent the rest of the night washing dishes with Grandma sitting on a chair nearby, her cane gripped with both hands in front of her. Whenever the dishwater got overly greasy, Grandma commanded us to throw it out the back door and fill the pan with boiling water from the whistling teakettle on the stove. She was always afraid the drains would plug up, knowing full well that even in those days, calling in a plumber would bring an impossible expense. After we got the kitchen in shipshape order Howard and Day went to bed. I stayed up with Grandma until Ma's return, once again sharing their beloved coffee and sugar lump dunking ritual.

Wash day was Ma's assignment. I often helped by pushing the ancient copper washer out into the middle of the kitchen floor and filling pan after pan of water for heating on the less than effective gas burners. Once the washer tub was filled and began to shimmy, Ma and I would take a coffee break. The long process was repeated through the rinsing cycle, each step culminating in the removal of the stuffed-rag-stopper and the draining into a huge copper vat positioned just below the missing stopper spigot. The final delight for me was turning the ringer handle as Ma carefully inserted soaked portions of wash. Once done, with a handle of the wicker clothes basket of wet clothes in one each of our hands, we lugged the heavy load outside and clothes-pinned each piece across rotting clotheslines in the backyard. Though Ma never allowed me to carry the boiling pots of water to the washing machine, once when she was out of the room I thought I could hurry the process by taking on that task. As I crossed the room with the overloaded pot it sloshed onto my hand and flew from my grasp, a gush of boiling water spattering across my legs. My howls brought Grandma and Ma running. Grandma applied layer on layer of corn starch paste as Ma held me in her arms and calmed me. I was kept home in bed for a week after that disaster during which time I read *Les Miserables.* I recall Day and Howard, on return after school the day I finished that book, being astounded to find me lying in Grandma's bed overcome with hysterical sobs. They were sure I had suffered a terrible setback. I was in fact mourning the heart-wrenching destiny of Jean Valjean.

That first winter when we twins were nine and Day was eleven, in another attempt at mutiny with our ears glued to Grandma's table radio as we listened to *The Shadow,* Grandma tried to get our attention for some household task by shrieking, "Jeg skal slå deg til hoddet står fast i veggen!" (I'll beat you 'til your head stands in the wall!). We turned up the volume. Grandma stomped from the room, soon reappearing in her winter coat and hat, heading for the door. Pausing a moment she banged her cane against the floor and barked, "Jeg går nå og kommer ikke igjen!" (I'm going now and I won't be back!), then slammed the door shut behind her. My sister and I hunkered closer to the radio, Howard, barefoot and in his pajamas, leapt up and ran out after Grandma screaming, "Don't leave Grandma! Don't leave!" She hastily returned with Howard in tow, pulled him onto her lap and rubbed his cold wet feet between her hands. My sister and I, sheepish and ashamed, gathered around Grandma, hugging her and begging for forgiveness.

In spite of our on-going skirmishes with Grandma there was yet another favorable upshot from her call to arms. Ma was allowed to play her piano. Favorite pieces from her music stand were left out for use at dusk. Strains of "I'm Waiting For Ships That Never Come In," "Little Love Boat Come Back,

Come Back Into Port," and "Memories," echoed up the bare cracked walls to the high ceilings, filling the house with bliss. Even Grandma seemed soothed when Ma played her piano. At bedtime cocooned to my chin in heavy blankets, the music floated through the house and descended over me like a spring mist..."Little Love Ship Come Back, Come Back into Port, Come back with your treasure of gold..." My thoughts drifted with the music, exotic scenes of far off lands, lovers embracing on moonlit shores, transported me to sleep and a long-lasting favorite dream, wherein I save myself from some disastrous plight like being lost, by springing up and down three times and then levitating above the ground and finally, swooping and dipping over the dark and silent neighborhood, the night stars twinkling all around me.

Grandma's downstairs realm was the complete opposite of the four upstairs rooms. Though I don't remember the details of the move, I remember helping carry box on box of possessions upstairs and dumping them in one or another of the four bedrooms. Only one of those rooms had a bed in it, impossible for use, as it was overloaded with papers, books, pictures, dumped boxes of sewing material, errant shoes or broken toys. Listing rockers and chairs leaned against walls, outgrown clothes flung across their arms. There were no curtains on any of the windows, no rugs, no amenities Grandma never laid eyes on those upstairs rooms. It was Ma's domain, which she said she would someday organize into a cozy retreat for me and her. She never did.

Knowing Grandma was too arthritic to manage the stairs, Ma's bent for structured chaos held sway. And though she insisted, "I can always find what I'm looking for," she neglected to add, "...if push comes to shove." Ma was content to keep the doors closed on each mounting disaster. If Grandma, as was her wont from time to time, demanded sewing materials, or papers, or old photos and other cherished effects, Ma would hold her at bay with excuses. Then, when Grandma dozed, with index finger pressed to her lips, Ma silently nodded toward the hallway and with me following behind, we crept upstairs. Out of range of what would have certainly been a major volcanic eruption on Grandma's part at the spectacle, Ma ripped through the bursting-at-the-seams boxes and bags. She never bothered to repack anything, though the more Ma dumped and tossed, the more I stacked and sorted, during those frequent raids. I was forever on the lookout for Larsen belongings of the past and their accompanying fascinating sagas. Ma didn't much appreciate my attempts at order, often complained, "If you keep moving stuff around, I'll NEVER find a thing!"

I cleared the second floor landing by shoving excess boxes and furniture into the already overloaded bedrooms, then pushed Grandpa's Edison Victrola into the middle of that cracked linoleumed space. There, using the long landing rail as my *barre,* I practiced ballet exercises to Viennese waltzs from Grandpa's ancient and scratched record collection. At dusk I quickly vacated the area. I had come to believe a presence that only emerged at night, occupied the upper floor of that claptrap monstrosity. A long ago nightmare resides with me still. I dreamed a giant boa constrictor had me in his grip and was dragging me though the staircase door up into the darkness beyond.

I danced for Grandma on many occasions. She seemed to revel in my talent, no doubt content that the fifty-cents a week she supplied for my lessons was not being wasted. She especially loved it when Ma accompanied me on the piano with pieces from her innumerable sheet-music collection, like "The Blue Skirt Waltz." What with those performances and all the dancing I did upstairs, it's no wonder Ma held fast to a dream that I would become a famous ballerina. I didn't do as well with my violin and cello undertakings. The violin was the worst jolt to Grandma's sensitive hearing. I never could quite keep that instrument from squawking. During my less than adequate practice sessions Grandma shouted for moderation while covering her ears against the racket. When I gave violin up for cello, Grandma's reaction was not as dramatic, though she exhibited unusual amusement at my awkward positioning of that contraption between my legs, commenting to Ma, "Hun er så morsom" (She's so amusing). I finally quit the cello as well, finding it an impossible inconvenience to drag back and forth to school. During my involvement in our Girl Scout Drama Club, I at first thought Grandma's reaction encouraging. She seemed particularly delighted with my death scenes, though sometimes her responses were unexpected. Once, as I threw myself onto the sofa-bed wailing and writhing in the throes of agony, Grandma lapsed into convulsive laughter. I thought she was merely exhibiting her usual state of high agitation until Grandma's hysterical laugh faded and she broke into muffled sobbing, tears streaming down her cheeks. She was, no doubt, recalling Uncle Gunnar's youthful bent for drama, as out of the blue she said, "Jeg ville så gjerne se ham" (I would so love to see him). I knew in my bones exactly who she meant and immediately modified my emotional histrionics by rising from my death bed and bouncing into a lively Charleston routine.

Grandma's steel grip on our lives did not extend beyond the walls of the Hellesen duplex. She rarely went outside, for which we were eternally grateful, I'm afraid. We were sure our friends thought her an oddity, as few had a grandparent living with them. Still, we kids relied on Grandma to assuage our pain, whether physical or emotional. She would open her arms in invitation for us to lean down for a hug. And though Grandma's inability to control our outside activities sometimes was a plus, it also meant she seldom could exercise her strong sense of over-protectiveness on our behalf, brought home to me by my run-in with Merle Wallin, and later, Old Mac.

FUN AND GAMES

One dewy summer morning, I peddled my twin's bicycle west on Sixtieth Street toward the railroad depot past endless vacant lots overgrown with shoulder-high grasses and wild flowers. Approaching a copse of sagging, decaying trees, that we kids had dubbed "The Spot," Merle Wallin suddenly jumped from his hiding place there and grabbed the handlebars of the bicycle. Alarmed at the specter of Merle running off with Howard's bike and my twin's imagined reaction, I gripped the bars tight, my eyes fixed on Merle's badly bitten fingernails. I was fully aware of the reputation of the Wallin boys as unruly tempered bullies, but I figured Merle, the youngest of the tribe, was hardly a formidable threat. Two years younger than me, he had gimlet eyes and a continuously dripping nose which forever after prompted me to mentally brand him, "snot snout Wallin."

Much to my surprise Merle let loose his grip on the bike handles, grabbed me around the waist and tugged and pulled until I dropped the bike to fend him off. Barely five-feet tall, Merle seemed midget-like; his head just reached my chin. His intent quickly became apparent; Merle pulled me close and attempted to plant a kiss on my lips, fell short and grazed my chin with his sun-blistered lips. Convulsed with laughter by then, I pushed Merle away. He fell backward into the brush as I picked up the bicycle and ran for home.

I saw Merle at the Bryant All Class Reunion in 1982 and related that adventure to him. Tall and good-looking by then, Merle remembered nothing of the incident joked, "I wouldn't mind the chance to get you in the bushes now!" As we joined in laughter, together with his nearby, notably younger second wife, I felt an odd twinge of regret.

During the Hellesen years the Wallin boys lived on the fringe of our group of friends whose beaten tracks spread far and wide, like multi-pronged trails from the widest possible base to the end most calculable point of our front porch at Sixtieth Street and Oakes Avenue. It now occurs to me that perhaps, with no male authority apparent, they felt freer to release the pent-up prepubescent frenzy that seemed to infuse them. I thought those boys boisterous hell cats, throwing sticks and bits of bark and finally, good sized rocks at each other, bellowing obscene merriment, flicking buggers or bursting into uncontrollable cackles. Though often intolerable, I was drawn to them like a newborn calf to its mother's teat, my presence secured due to my status as Howard's twin, though often it was he who exiled me.

Howard and his friends Jerry Bibeau, Joe Fudally, Donald Richard Larson, Butch Lindner and Eddie Zelma took possession of our half of the dilapidated coal shed out back, dubbing it, The Shack and affixing a sign, KEEP OUT! My twin banned me from that private space, though I seldom cared, as those particular boys did not draw my affection as much as the older amongst our group, like the hazel-eyed and tawny complexioned Kendall Nelson. He treated me quite charitably due, I'm sure, to the fact his folks held a deep respect for Ma and Grandma. I recall Kendall once saying, "You're a real clever girl, Frances," his words intoxicating me for weeks after.

Walter Getschow, who lived at the end of the block north of us, drew my fascination as well. Though a bit gawky and loose-limbed, with a prominent Adam's apple, he had an open and respectful manner with females. Both Walter and Kendall had no doubt been well churched at Bethel, their parents stalwart supporters of family values, resulting in those boys refraining from the more raucous antics of the other boys.

Howard's bulky, square-faced friend Jerry Bibeau, who lived in a converted storefront building on Fifty-Ninth Street and Tower Avenue, like many of the boys in that era, had a crew-cut. I remember his bandy-legged, wiry father who trained German Shepherds in his spare time and was much friendlier and outgoing than his son. Jerry's eyes seemed forever averted, as he stood feet apart, hands permanently sunk in his pants pockets or clasped behind his back, like an Army drill sergeant.

Joe Fudally and his brother Bobby; were our closest friends geographically. They lived in the first house beyond the vacant lot next door to us. Carrot topped and freckled, Joe blushed a lot, had jug ears and was often overcome by fits of laughter. He was good at sports, played on Bryant School's basketball team, and later played intramural sports in high school. His widowed father had remarried; I remember Ma commenting that Joe resembled his deceased mother.

Bobby, two years our junior, was an outgoing, clear-eyed and puckish boy. He bubbled and sparkled, though his high-pitched cackle was an irritation, as well as his habit of tagging behind us girls when the older boys didn't want to be bothered with him. Then Bobby would run his bicycle up on our porch sending us flying in all directions and bringing Grandma to the window shaking her fist. Bobby grew up to become a bank vice president. I used to stop and see him when I was in town from Chicago and though his impressive brass nameplate said ROBERT Fudally, I could never bring myself to call him anything but Bobby and still do.

Donald Richard Larson was Howard's best friend. He lived in the next block north of us. I don't recall ever seeing his parents and didn't even know that Don had older siblings until years later. I do remember the large Catholic Kenville family kitty-corner across the street from him. It was rumored amongst the Lutherans that Mrs. Kenville got a medal from the Pope for having so many children. A bubbling-over madcap most of the time, Don had a booming horse laugh. He was a gangly boisterous sort, though never menacing. His spiky unmanageable hair and ever wet lips splaying spittle when he talked, were abhorrent to me, though I admired his jaunty attitude.

Don and Howard loved a good prank, though often their antics ended in one kind of mess or other. One Halloween when the street light was out at our intersection, they built a barricade and were chased by an irate foot patrolman. I remember my twin bursting through the kitchen door and running pell-mell for the toilet upstairs. The rank odor emanating from his baggy corduroys clued us into the extent of his disaster, doubly humiliating to Howard as the sultry, doe-eyed Josie Crusher, who adored him, was present.

Howard's other hangers-on included Butch Lindner, a pouty, lantern jawed boy, from Central Avenue near the depot and Eddie Zelma, whose family lived on the other side of the Fudallys. Eddie was rather nondescript, though I do remember his sandy-red hair. He and Jimmy Jacovetti were often the odd boys out in the games and antics that pervaded the group's summer fun. Jimmy lived on the east side of Tower Avenue; his mother was my Girl Scout leader. A badger-like slight, dark-eyed and large nosed boy, Jimmy stood out as the most expert jester and cackler of Howard's riotous crew.

We were sure all those boys puffed on Lucky Strike or Camel cigarettes in The Shack, as my girlfriends and I could smell the smoke when we played *Inne-inne-eye-over*, tossing a ball over that shed and after catching it, running with it to tag members of the opposing team. We never squealed on them though, as we ourselves were experimenting with dry weeds rolled in toilet paper at The Spot.

Howard and his friends played football in the empty lot next to our building, as well. On occasion they would let Lois and me join in. I suspected it was because they all idolized my ivory-complexioned pretty friend, though she was as less-than-athletic as me, with her slightly knocked-knees and awkward left throwing hand. It nettled me to see them tackle her more often than me, rolling over the ground with Lois in their arms for what seemed an eternity. When at age thirteen, I got *the curse,* Ma gave me her capsuled sex education lecture, the only part of which I remember was that I shouldn't participate in physical activity. I recall standing on the football sidelines while Howard and his friends skirmished back and forth with Lois, all the while taunting me to join in. The longer I stood idle the more fearful I became, sure that the sanitary napkin between my legs, which felt like an oversized cushion, was visible to one and all. Verging on tears, I would eventually run home into Grandma Larsen's comforting arms.

That monthly visitor, as Ma called menstruation, was particularly demeaning when our supply of Kotex ran out. It seemed to me that I was always the one delegated to go to the drugstore on Fifty-Ninth and Tower for the restocking. There, flushed and nervous, I would have to tell the male clerk which of the color-coded wrapped boxes I wanted. I recall that the size I used was camouflaged in violet paper. I was sure the clerk leered at me when he handed it over. If that wasn't bad enough, there was always a clutch of swarthy faced male peers hanging out on that corner. One or the other of them always broke into a singsong chant, "We know what you bought!"

What with all the boys who gathered on our sagging front porch with its rung-less railings, my girlfriends found it an ideal site for flitting and flirting in high-pitched silliness. Besides Lois, from a block away came Doris Raulerson, Donna Sands, the Kersten sisters and sometimes Mary Ann Schneeberger, who bicycled from six blocks north of us. I'm positive the Kersten girls were merely exhibiting innocent curiousness as they were devout Bethel Church member friends. Like the Noeth sisters, they were as different as night and day; Helen the oldest, was stocky and dark, Janet slender and light. I spent hours playing hop scotch and skipping rope with them.

I recall a couple occasions when Betty Jane Hannum, our landlord's step daughter and Vivien Raulerson, Doris' sister, sunbathed on a blanket alongside our building. I felt particularly honored to be included by those older girls as I was in awe of their profuse cleavage, partially revealed by the skimpy halter tops they wore. For days after I would inspect my own breasts, hoping against hope that one day I too would be as abundantly endowed.

We three girls fantasized about roaming the U.S.A. together in a Silver Stream trailer attached to Mr. Hellesen's Ford coupe.' Betty and her new groom, married shortly after Betty's high-school graduation, were killed in a head-on collision on their honeymoon trip in Texas.

I spent many hours in the Helleson's apartment dancing for old Mrs. Hannum, a fragile, stooped, and gnome-like woman who was Mrs. Hellesen's ninety-year-old mother-in-law. It took years for me to understand that Betty's father had abandoned his family and that Mr. Hellesen was her stepfather. Mr. Hellesen worked at the creamery in South Superior and was fond of Howard. He took him to Trinity Methodist Church father and son banquets. Howard thought him kind and generous, but dull.

Our group of friends sometimes included my baby-sitting charges, the Bergs: Sandra and Doug, who were lumpish, flat-featured children, and Ronnie and Mickey, towheaded, delicate boys. I never enjoyed baby-sitting and found many of my wards uncontrollable devils. The Bergs were particularly difficult as it was often impossible for me to get them to go to bed. I dubbed them The Berg Brats.

I recall deciding one night that I could scare them into submission, crept into their darkened bedroom, charged to the window and pulled the shade as far down as it would go, then released it. It spun around and clattered to the floor. The Berg brats screamed, "You broke it! You broke it! We're going to tell our ma!" On another occasion I blasted in swinging a broom over my head. The broom hit the overhead light fixture and shattered it. Years later Ronnie Berg told my brother that the Berg Brats all thought I was crazy.

Mrs. Berg, a petite, delightfully sweet and lighthearted woman, with a mischievous look about her, was divorced from her alcoholic husband and was dating one of the Chesky bachelors. Mr. Berg showed up banging on the door one night when I was in charge. I refused to open it to him on instruction of Mrs. Berg. Their kids screamed and cried for their father, but I held fast, even when that forbidding, mammoth man staggered from window to window whopping and thundering so hard against the panes I was sure they would break. Frantic, I called Ma; she came over and talked him into leaving. Ma felt sorry for Mr. Berg as, "He came from such fine Norwegian stock." I guess she felt her intervention that night was just cause for filling our coal bucket with briquettes from Mrs. Berg's supply, too. I was appalled by Ma's action, though I too was slipping into the morass of hypocrisy.

A few times, after the Berg brats were asleep, I invited one or another of my current targets of misplaced affection over to keep me company. I recall rolling about on top of Mrs. Berg's unmade bed with all my clothes on, though the physical act if any and my coconspirators identities remain clouded by time.

In the late 1980s a childhood cohort of my twin's, stranded at O'Hare Airport in Chicago, called me and we met for dinner. Several cocktails into the meal he matter-of-factly said, "You were the first for me," his remark preceded by the admission during our reminiscing on childish romances, of a lifelong crush on the athletic, serene and popular Inez Lizdahl. I blurted, "Belly rubbing between little girls and boys doesn't count." I must have hurt his feelings as later, when I put him up for the night, he quickly rebuffed me on suggestion that we repeat the act, mumbling, "I'm a happily married man." My ruffled feathers were sufficiently smoothed the next morning after he installed a ceiling fan for me before he returned to O'Hare and resumed his cancelled flight.

On occasion I kept Betty Jane Hannum company on her baby-sitting duties at the Kenbok house on Butler avenue, behind Fudally's house. Betty and I worked for hours on our and the docile Janet's, homework assignments. Janet Kenbok was a dark haired little beauty whose infant brother Ronnie slept a lot and was even more obedient than Janet. Ronnie died from a burst appendix while a third grader. Fellow Bryant students and I attended his funeral at Holy Assumption Catholic Church. The whole time there I worried about what our Lutheran minister would think, as we had been taught never to set foot in any church of a conflicting denomination. I remember sitting glued to the church pew during the lengthy funeral mass and strange rituals. My nervousness was compounded by a long-ago event, related to me by Ma. She told me that years before, Holy Assumption Church had been consumed by fire. Because it was April Fool's Day, no one believed the news until too late.

I enjoyed baby sitting the long-legged and alabaster skinned Judy Zimmerman, as her parents were a bit tipsy when they returned, resulting in Mr. Zimmerman overpaying me. After the Zimmermans moved, the Setterstoms occupied that house. Sue was the same age as me and was quickly welcomed into my circle of friends. A pigtailed, perpetually sun-bronzed girl, she was a tomboy who loved horses and galloped up and down Oakes Avenue neighing and nickering. I recall a tent in her backyard where she, Howard and I puffed on cigarettes, filling that space with clouds of smoke. I once slept over with Sue; her mother insisted I wash my feet before I crawled into bed.

I recall Patsy Grey, a sassy wan, sloe-eyed girl that I baby-sat. One Saturday afternoon I went to her house to collect my wages. The hefty Mrs. Grey was washing clothes in a wraparound kimono. When she leaned down to pick up a pile of clothes from the kitchen floor one of her breasts fell out. I was overcome with heat at the sight, which brought to mind the maxim, "Don't let your tit get caught in a ringer." I have no idea if Mrs. Grey was widowed or divorced, but was aware of the doll-like cozy ambiance her small, three-room house exuded. I thought it scandalous when I heard that one summer night, when everyone's windows were wide open, a drunk got into Mrs. Grey's bedroom, crawled under her covers and fell asleep without rousing her. The next morning in horrific shock, Mrs. Grey called the police and the drunk was hauled off to jail.

I filled in for my sister from time to time and baby-sat at the Andersons. They had three little boys and a girl at the time.

The two oldest, Orlan and Johnny, were regular visitors at our house. Ma was especially fond of Orlan, a singular bright boy who carried on conversations like an adult. He became a school official in a northern Wisconsin town. I don't know what became of Johnny or the other children, but recall that Johnny often felt compelled to run from his house naked and wallow in puddles of muddy water. Mr. Anderson was a cabdriver, Mrs. Anderson a nurse and hyperactive housekeeper who used gallon on gallon of bleach for cleaning. The fumes were so overwhelming they brought tears to my eyes.

Our main group of friends spent evenings playing hide and seek. I never went too far afield and often hid behind the home tree-trunk, unable to conquer my fear of darkness. Daytime hikes and picnics to the Pokegama River and Billings Drive were constants in summer. I only recall one birthday party in the Hellesen house, in 1946. Aunt Ethel was recruited to keep order. She taught us to play spin-the-bottle and post office, finding it quite amusing to have Ronnie Sands and me demonstrate the art of kissing. I remember standing at the top of the front stairs with Ronnie, lights ablaze, as we kissed and embraced like spotlighted movie stars. Even Grandma was amused by our antics.

She was not however, amused, the night I came home crying after my encounter with the Waltenberg girls. Rushing home at dusk from an errand to Sather's Grocery store, two of the girls jumped out of the shadows behind Old Mac's barbershop and grabbed me. I was sure I was in for a good pounding as they overpowered me and dragged me around the corner into the dark. Instead, I was pushed to my knees and somehow shoved into the barber's vacant dog house. As I burst into tears, the girls, reeling in laughter, commanded me to bark like a dog. The commotion brought lights in the upstairs apartment windows and the girls ran off. I didn't waste a second crawling out and running home in the opposite direction.

My skirmish with Old Mac was much more frightening.

OLD MAC

I had been warned. Ma distinctly stated, "When you get to old Mac's barber shop don't go in unless he has customers."

My twin Howard, didn't want to do his paper route collections. "Bad enough I have to deliver the papers," he said.

Our sister spouted, "Don't expect ME to go. I'm sick of doing his job."

Their gaze simultaneously fell on me. They knew I was always willing to tag alongside Ma on any errand. But she was lying on the couch, bathed in a cloud of pungent vinegar fumes. She was having another headache. I sensed her uneasiness at the thought of entrusting a rather frenetic thirteen-year-old with as big a responsibility as asking for money. But Grandpa was gone and Grandma was resigned to less weighty tasks than problem solving. Tough decisions had become a fact of life for Ma. Besides, we all knew that the collected monies would have to be used for groceries, to be reimbursed on the first of the month from her sixty dollar alimony/child support check or Grandma's paltry old age pension, so someone had to go.

I set out more concerned about making change for the inevitable dollar bills my twin's customers extended. Counting nickels and dimes and pennies was not one of my better talents. By the third or fourth house down from home base I'd gotten the hang of it and was feeling pretty smug as I savored the chocolate chip cookie I'd gotten from Mrs. Peterson.

I tripped along until up ahead, I saw Old Mac's barber pole. The setting sun reflected in jagged rays off the bright red, white and blue stripes that wound endlessly up and down, round and round. Ma's warning suddenly burst into my head..."Don't go into Old Mac's barbershop unless there's customers...." I gingerly approached the white picket fence that bordered two small flower beds in front of the barbershop, then halted in mid-track. It occurred to me that Ma didn't say <u>why</u> I shouldn't go in. She <u>never</u> seemed to explain things, though once when Old Mac's name came up Ma and Grandma glanced at each other as if they knew a secret about him which they didn't pursue. At least not in front of us kids.

I leaned towards the plate glass front window, saw Old Mac stretched back in his barber chair, legs crossed, the evening paper spread over his face. There was not a customer in sight.

My eyes slowly searched the small room and I saw the curtained door beyond. I guessed that was where the old man slept, as the apartment next door was where my nemesis Doris Raulerson lived and I was sure the layout was the same. Perhaps someone was using the bathroom that would be located there. Besides, I had seen Old Mac sitting out front chatting with passersby, or to Doris and her mother and sister. He always waved and sang out a cheery "Hi," to us neighborhood kids. What could possibly be wrong with such a friendly old man? I skipped up the two low flat front stairs, opened the door and entered. A tinkling bell announced my presence.

"Well, well, who have we got HERE?" Old Mac lowered his paper and grunted to his feet. "Aren't you one of the Oliphant twins?"

"My brother's sick, I came to collect for the paper," I said, assuming what I imagined was a businesslike stance - my fisted hands on my hips, a frown darkening my face - much like Grandma's stance when she meant business. All the time I was thinking that if I didn't stay long, I wouldn't be ignoring Ma's warning and she couldn't get angry with me.

Old Mac walked over to his huge oak cash register, pressed hard on a button and after the drawer shot open, pulled out a five dollar bill. I felt heat rise on my neck as I frantically tried to calculate the change that huge bill would require. Old Mac loomed toward me, his pasty, loose-skinned face and bulbous nose barely visible above his huge frame with its distended flabby stomach. His thumb was behind a suspender strap, the five dollar bill partially caught in his grip. "Can you make change?" he asked, leaning over me. I felt a creepy sensation, like crawling ants, seize me as he edged closer. His face seemed wet, his eyes strangely bright.

Something sank inside as it dawned on me that Old Mac <u>knew</u> I didn't know how to make change. He stepped closer, "Let me get the change." In a flash he lurched forward, pulled me against his massive body and slid his hand down inside my pant leg pocket. It felt like a hot flat iron pressing and probing as his fleshy paw moved, not to the coins and bills at the base of the pouch, but toward my inner thigh. His Old Spice cologne engulfed me like a rolling fog as Old Mac's frog-like face lowered to mine and his wet mouth locked on my lips. I felt saliva drip onto my neck; I jerked back, felt material tear, heard nickels and dimes clatter across his polished linoleum floor. "Let me go!" I shrieked.

"Don't holler," Old Mac said. "I'll get you the right change. It's in the back, come on, it'll just be a second." He turned as if to move away, and then his sweaty hand shot out and gripped me by my wrist.

"Let **go!**" I screeched.

"Sssh," Old Mac stage-whispered as he turned toward the curtained door tugging me behind. My mind began churning out movie screen images of overwrought heroines in distress. "Wait," I said, "...maybe someone'll...come in. I could ...come back later...when you're closed." Old Mac loosened his grip. I immediately bolted for the door. I could hear him calling behind me, "Don't forget. <u>Tonight</u>." Without losing a beat in my fast-paced gallop home I turned my head, heard my tear-choked shout, **"I'm going to tell my mother on you!"**

At home, on hearing my sobbing recital, Grandma slammed her cane on the library table, "Stygg gammel mann!" (Dirty old man!). Ma jumped up from her sick bed. I could hear her on the phone relating my adventure to the police woman, Miss Lindstrom. And though I wasn't interviewed by the police, years later Ma told me that she and Miss Lindstrom made a visit to the barbershop. At the time I was just relieved that Ma wasn't angry with me. Forever after I crossed the street to avoid any contact with Old Mac.

I noticed a peculiar upshot from that adventure, while relating the story to the ever-anxious-for-salacious-details, Doris. I seemed to have become a significant personage in her eyes. She hung on my words at each tidbit, the pale irises in her watery eyes dilating, though like me, she could not know or imagine what meaning lie behind Old Mac's actions. She seemed disappointed, wrestled for control in her take-charge-manner and said, "You should have yelled for me or banged on the wall."

Vexed, I snapped, "I didn't know <u>what</u> to do for criminally sakes!"

Though irritated with her, Doris' celebrity-like attention and concern had thrilled me and brought with it the beginning of a notion that people noticed you when you shocked them.

QUESTIONS

My father loved to go down to St. Louis Bay to fish. Alone. I discovered that fact at age thirteen. Since age eight, when he'd visited at the old Kronlund House and suddenly pulled me to him and kissed my neck and began to tickle me, I had put the memory of that stocky stranger behind me. During that wartime visit, unable to be consoled by my father's coos and kisses, I had burst into tears. Breaking away I stared at him as if to imprint his clear-faced good looks on my memory as he covered and uncovered his face with his hands, reciting in a singsong voice, "Now you see me, now you don't." Five years later, when I asked Ma why he had left I didn't get an answer at first.

It happened one evening after playing with my best friend Lois in the Paul's kitchen. Still smarting from Mrs. Paul's questions - "Where's your father?" "Are your parents divorced?" I burst into the living room and slammed the door behind me. Ma lay bundled in an Afghan on the lumpy hide-a-bed we shared. I quickly kissed her and then stood back from the familiar vinegar odor that rose from a cloth on her forehead. A spate of irritation rose as I demanded, "Why did my father leave?"

"Not now," Ma said. "I have a spitting headache. Tomorrow." I felt a lump form in my throat as I thought of the closeness we shared, remembered Ma's concern just a week earlier after my encounter with Old Mac. Ma had pulled me into her arms and wailed, "My God...when I think what could have...oh, God. Don't ever go near that barbershop again!" The aroma of her Desert Flower cologne had washed over me, dispelling old Mac's image.

The next night I rushed in again. The setting sun shown dull through the sooty living room windows and stagnant vinegar fumes still lay on the air. Ma sat cross-legged on the floor surrounded by open boxes brimming with tangled clothes, snapshots and papers. She handed me a small file-card covered with cramped, minuscule handwriting. "Your father wrote this. Keep it."

I tramped into the kitchen where Grandma stood in front of the grease caked gas-stove muttering and stirring a huge kettle of vegetable soup. Grandma's muttering was an on-going complaint that I thought peculiar. It seemed as if she repeated the complaint so much she had memorized it and then forgot what it was about.

"Hi, Grandma!" I sang out. She kept on muttering and stirring as I kissed her wrinkled cheek and sat on a stool nearby to read to myself: *I walk alone and on the street I chance to meet some person that I know I tip my hat and chew the fat and then I walk alone. Down to the bay I go each day to fish or hunt or trap, In rain or snow I always go and always walk alone. For blondes so fair I do not care, I'll take a short brunette, So sweet and kind and quick of mind, I'm looking for her yet.*

And when I die as you and I will have to do some day, I'll leave behind this quest of mine, I hope I'm still alone.

My father's poem did not make sense to me. I had light-colored hair, Ma's was dark. I was sure we were sweet and kind and quick of mind, too.

I asked Grandma, "Did you like my father?"

Grandma took off her steamed glasses and wiped them on her long paisley apron.

""Han var umulig" (He was no good).

"I hate him!" I blurted.

Grandma bent down and hugged me. "Ja, det gjør du sikkert" (Yah, I'm sure you do). Her plumpness felt toasty-warm, like in winter when I'd come in half frozen and Grandma would put my hands under her armpits to heat them.

That same week I asked Aunt Ethel, "Why did my father run away?"

"He was never a family man. It was all wrong for him," she answered.

126

I was sure that Aunt Ethel blamed Ma for everything. Sometimes I wondered if she blamed us kids, too. That made me feel helpless inside, like when I got promoted and my twin was held back. It didn't stop me, though. Whenever I got the chance I badgered Ma with questions. Once, as she fixed her languid sad eyes on mine Ma said, "Curiosity killed a cat."

Grandma countered in a snappish voice, "La henne vare. Hun er en lur pike, stiller alltid spørsmal, men svarer ikke på noen" (She's a smart girl, always asking questions but never answering any).

I couldn't find the nerve to ask Ma or Grandma new questions that plagued me, though. The questions began to form after a visit to newly married Cousin Peggy Larson. Spotting a long cord embedded in a bar of soap hanging from a hook on her bathroom door, I was sure it was some kind of gadget used to help make babies. None of the true confession magazines that Cousin Teedie Wiberg gave me, had the answer. The stories all ended before the imagined scene. The longed for vision faded in thundering music and exploding fireworks in the few romantic films featured at the Beacon or Palace Theaters. My twin, like most of the boys our age, seemed only interested in tricks and teasing. I couldn't ask my sister. She always had her nose in a book and when pestered, would stare at me as if I were a freak and not say a word. My days seemed to be overflowing with baffling riddles and confusing merriment.

I was developing into a flat-chested adolescent, short and with what I thought were piano legs and spindly arms. I took to wearing bright red lipstick from a discarded tube I had found in the street. Often I quickly wiped it off with the back of my hand before entering school or returning home. I would explain away the smeared results to Ma as stains from plums or strawberries I had eaten at the Paul's house.

My face was pale like Ma's, but not as silky and smooth. Bouts of acne were a constant torment. I spent hours with a magnifying mirror squeezing white heads until they popped.

My hair, often so tightly braided that my eyes turned up at the corners, prompted my twin to dub me Tokyo-Rose.

It felt as if something was smoldering inside, like the banked fire in our living room heater whose hot pulsing coals I sometimes starred at so long tears came to my eyes. It was a moody energy, a restless trancelike longing for something hidden. I would catch myself standing motionless, then would walk on, stop and stare into space. I'd have to kick at the earth with my toe to snap out of the sensation before I could continue on. At other times I would be snapped awake by the calls and yells from neighborhood boys playing sandlot baseball. I would wander to the lot then and stand transfixed. I yearned to be near males; I craved their attention.

One day, while riding Howard's bike, I saw Walter Getchow and his father approach. Walter was one of a myriad of boys I had crushes on. He gained prominence on the list when he accidentally touched my breast one summer evening as a bunch of neighborhood kids and I rolled on the grass. I had been driven to kiss Walter on the lips. He jumped to his feet and ran home with catcalls and laughter trailing after him. As Walter and his father neared, I felt the bike's front wheel weave and bounce and then, settle between Walter's long legs. I dropped the bike and ran home, my hot face wet with tears. Later, remembering that encounter, a tingling filled my breasts.

I began hovering near the pool hall where dull-eyed boys lazed in front of the building. They wore black leather jackets and engineers' boots that reflected the sun. Pall Mall cigarettes dangled from their wet lips as they yelled out the side of their mouths at the girls who crossed the street to avoid them. I stood apart and kept watch until one or another of them jumped into his souped up car, gunned the motor and sped away in a roar of cinders and smoke. I would feel a heavy sigh rise up then and would turn and wander home. At other times I stared transfixed by the occasional grown-up male who entered my world, like Reverend Zoarb.

128

Reverend Ernest Zoarb assumed the pastoral duties at Bethel Lutheran church in 1948, his first post since discharge from a stint in the US Army as a hospital chaplain. The church board no doubt expected the usual quiet, unassuming pastor. Reverend Zoarb did not fit the bill. From the first Sunday when his bombastic style became apparent, hastily called meetings were set into motion. Many believed that Reverend Zoarb wasted a lot of time, "teaching our boys and girls physical education." Others objected, "I don't like them tramping through the woods taking pictures of birds, either. Sounds like sissy business to me." When whispers reached Reverend Zoarb's ears of, "uncomely activity befitting a man of the cloth," he gave a sermon on Sodom and Gomorra, his deep bass voice echoing off the eves of the church. "For we will destroy this place, because the cry of them is waxen and the Lord hath sent us to destroy it!"

Once in my wanderings, I trailed behind a group of the pastor's acolytes as they made their way to the church basement. Descending the stairs, I saw Reverend Zoarb standing on his head clothed in Army fatigue pants and a green T-shirt. My eyes fixed on his bare, muscular shoulders. Frozen like a statue, my mouth agape, the pastor suddenly jumped up and said, "Come join us, Frances." My face burned as I roused myself and thundered up the stairs gasping for breath. Reverend Zoarb's bare shouldered image blazed in my mind's eye. The following Sunday I enrolled in the junior confirmation class, burrowing into religion as if it were a treasure chest at the bottom of a narrow chasm. I was determined to dazzle the pastor and pledge my life to God. Grandma's sudden illness helped steel my determination.

On April 2, 1948 I wrote in my diary: *Grandma was fixing supper and had a stroke. Her hands were limp, her wedding ring fell off. It rolled across the floor. I had to sleep with Day. I don't think Grandma is sane.*

Then on April third: *To Confirmation class. To Lange's Bakery & shoemaker. Helped Grandma to her chair. Mrs.*

Hellesen came later to help Ma. I went to dance lesson, home. They took Grandma to the hospital. To bed 11 p.m. On April fourth I went to the hospital with Ma. My diary entry reads: *"Grandma looked just awful. It made me cry."* I never visited Grandma again. She lingered five more days without knowing or responding to any of us and then died alone. Her passing brought more questions to my mind.

As my twin and I sat on either side of Ma waiting for the funeral service to begin I asked, "Is there a heaven?"

"Ask the minister," Ma answered.

Twisting the ribbon on the bodice of my best dress I leaned forward and looked at Howard. I wanted to be sure he hadn't heard. By then I had begun to detest my twin's habitual teasing. Just that morning as I was reading, <u>Little Women</u> waiting for Ma to get ready, my twin hissed, "I got a better book for you, 'The Open Kimono,' by I. Seymour Hare. It's very revealing." I flushed with anger, threw my book at him. It glanced off Howard's forehead. He howled when he felt a fine line of blood form. Ma jumped off her vanity stool so fast it toppled. As she rushed forward, clad only in her slip, I noticed the dark patch of hair that shown through. Wondering then why I had no hair, I slid my hand down the front of my dress and pressed myself.

Ma shrieked, "Stop that!," pulled my hand away and slapped it. Just as suddenly she sobbed, "I'm sorry, I'm sorry." Her muffled words sounded hollow and I felt my own eyes fill.

Later, sitting in the funeral parlor I felt uneasy, like the time Grandma screeched a wife's tale warning, "Svelg ikke de stenen; da kommer et tre til å vokse ut av hodet på deg" (Don't swallow those seeds: a tree will grow out of the top of you head), and I had felt under my pinned-up braids for the bump. My uneasiness began the night before when Reverend Zoarb came to our house to pray with us. I was so absorbed in staring at him that I hadn't cried for Grandma. A tall and pale man of forty or so, Reverend Zoarb had skin as smooth as one of my twin's agates. His take-charge bearing, added to the attraction.

A quick rustling of cloth roused me. I looked up to see Reverend Zoarb standing at the funeral parlor lectern. A strange ache moved to my throat and then below my heart and I could hear the sound of my blood pound through me. I lowered my head for the opening prayer. When I raised it Reverend Zoarb's somber brown eyes momentarily rested on mine. In the flutter of strange longing that touched me, I forgot to cry for Grandma again.

Later, standing amongst the mourners in the damp mist that shrouded Riverside cemetery, I watched as the coffin was lowered. Without warning I felt tears gush. Reverend Zoarb gently lay his hand on my shoulder. I turned and flung my arms around his waist. The fabric of his black vestment felt rough against my face and smelled pungent with tobacco. The aroma swelled through me as I heard him intone a line from the hymn that had been sung for Grandma...*and the joy we share, as we tarry there, none other has ever known.*

At the luncheon that followed, I began to formulate a question in my mind about heaven for Reverend Zoarb. A different one burst out, "Do you believe in divorce?"

"No," he answered.

I couldn't understand why Ma got upset. I was happy I had got an answer. Reverend Zoarb had all the answers and I was sure he would share them with me.

At home I announced, "I've found Jesus."

"I didn't know he was lost," my twin hooted. "You just want to get on the good side of that minister. You're man-crazy. Why lie?"

I threw a pillow at him and ran upstairs. Kicking through the boxes and collapsing bags of old newspapers and magazines, I pushed into one of the four unoccupied bedrooms. I had claimed that private space early in our move to the Hellesen house. There, after shoving past broken furniture, splitting boxes and bags of belongings from our hasty move, I threw myself on the single mattress I had lain on the floor under the lone window. It was there I found the privacy I had come to hunger for and was unable to find downstairs. Both my twin and my sister thought the upstairs was haunted. I had my doubts, though I did take the precaution of spending only day-lit hours up there. It was the perfect time of day to allay any suspicion that I was doing anything nasty, as my twin called things sexual. What it did create was the thought that I was bound for the fires of hell.

Still, from then through the following year, I attended confirmation classes, doted on the minister and rose to the top of my class. On Sunday mornings I scoured the neighborhood for children to drag to Sunday school. None of my enthusiasm rubbed off on my mother or my siblings. Once Ma said, "I can't bear that minister. He thinks divorce is a deadly sin. Like it was my fault."

It reminded me of Reverend Zoarb's sermon censuring divorce. When he boomed, "What God has joined together, let no man put asunder," I crunched down in my front pew seat unable to move. Then I closed my eyes tight and prayed that Reverend Zoarb wouldn't blame me for my parents' action.

Ma's disinterest hardened my resolve. I joined the Luther League and Donna Ely's *Sunshine Girls,* a group of nine to fourteen year old girls, who tramped through the woods along Billings Drive and sang our joy to God: *...Do not wait until some deed of greatness you may do... Do not wait to shed your light afar... To the many duties near you now be true. Brighten the corner where you are.*

Our joy was abruptly interrupted one Sunday afternoon when a man appeared on a knoll above our campsite, dropped his trousers and exposed himself. For an instant I felt an uncontrollable urge to rush up the hill and question him. Halted by the screams of my Sunshine companions, I broke camp with them and fled.

The religious fervor that possessed me spilled over into everything I did. In the autumn of 1949 when I started high school, I dove into the work like a champion swimmer covetous of a gold metal and received top billing on the freshman class honor roll that first semester.

Reverend Zoarb cited me in front of the congregation for my accomplishment. I rose from my front row seat on the burnished oak pew to acknowledge the applause that rang in my ears like a flourish of trumpets. When it subsided, I heard the last few words of the pastor's biblical pronouncement. "...and love conquers all." My gaze settled on his beaming face and I imagined a celestial light passed between us.

The week before the confirmation ceremony my classmates and I were summoned to the church for Reverend Zoarb's lecture on the facts of life. I was ecstatic, sure that all my questions would be answered, my prayers fulfilled.

Mrs. Zoarb and two Alter Guild ladies were dusting in the church nave as our group of three girls and five boys perched on the front pew. I was cheered by the sight of Mrs. Zoarb's plainness yet intrigued by the fact of her pregnant state. "How could he," I thought, completely ignorant of what exactly he had done. At the same time lines from a True Confessions article filled my head. They instructed wives to keep up their looks for their husbands if they want to keep them. "Husbands with plain wives deserve to be free," I thought. The revelation confirmed a suspicion that I had begun to formulate: Ma alone was to blame for father's desertion.

One by one the boys in the class were called into the pastor's office first. As each exited I stared at their faces, hoping their eyes would tell me the things I longed to know. It was no use. Each came out more red-faced than the last and all avoided my gaze. The girls, Shirley and Joanne, after their turns, seemed subdued and embarrassed. I didn't waste my pity on them though, due to a recent injury inflicted on me and recorded in my diary: *This morning at confirmation Shirley J. gave Joanne G. a stick of bubble gum, but not me.*

When it was my turn I stepped into the pastor's office as if I had taken possession. Sitting on a wing-back chair directly in front of the his mammoth desk, the aroma from newly varnished woodwork made me light-headed and I felt pearls of sweat form on my upper lip. I became aware of the thudding of my heart as the vapors seemed to engulf me and draw me closer to the object of my longing.

The pastor pulled open his desk drawer, took out a sheet of white bond paper and smoothed it with his pale hand. Each movement sent my heart soaring in a flight of drum thumping anticipation. I squirmed in the chair.

Reverend Zoarb picked up his fountain pen, dipped it in the crystal ink well on his shiny, uncluttered desk. He began to scratch a figure on the paper. The lines grew, sharp and black. My breasts pressed against the hard edge of the desk, my body strained in concentration. The pastor was drawing an apple.

"The simplest explanation of reproduction comes from the Bible. You Frances, I know, will have no difficulty understanding. Take your mind back to the Garden of Eden, to the apple —remembering always God the father, who loves us all."

I raised my eyes and tried to will the pastor to meet my gaze. He didn't. A pinpoint of doubt seemed focused inside, expanding like a red balloon.

"One only has to cut the apple in half to learn the secret of life." Reverend Zoarb picked up an apple that lay in a wicker basket on the desk. In one quick stroke he cut the fruit in half with a bronze letter-opener; a seed shot out in a splay of juice.

I felt something inside deflate as I slumped back into the chair.

"Behold a sower went forth to sow...and seeds fell by the wayside..."

His words transfixed me, though they seemed like echoes from stones cast into a bottomless well. *"...but other seeds fell into good ground and brought forth fruit..."*

I felt my fists clench and grow white at the knuckles. My gaze fixed on a spot on the flowered wallpaper just beyond the pastor's shoulder.

"...for all flesh is as grass and all the glory of man as the flower of grass. The grass withereth and the flower thereof falleth away..."

A chill played on the air around me and shadows danced over the heavy furniture. I shivered and bolted upright as the door banged open. Reverend Zoarb's words abruptly ended. His wife stood framed in the light from beyond the room. "Are you through, dear?" she asked.

"In a moment." He rose to help her with the tray. "We decided that the star pupil should have a special treat," he continued, touching his wife's swollen belly and kissing her lightly on her cheek.

With his wife standing alongside, her hand on his shoulder, Reverend Zoarb finished his lesson... *"The sinner may be deeper in sin than the depths of Hell itself, but the love of the Father can reach him still..."* As he continued his voice seemed to be coming from far away, as if smothered in layers of crinoline. *"The hope of salvation lies with God, our father.* Have you any questions?"

Bile rose in my throat and I tensed with a sudden desire to cry. I closed my eyes tight, tried to hold back the tears, but could not. I heard myself holler, "FATHER? I have no father!!!" Jumping to my feet I rushed to the door, pulled it open and ran from the church.

A week later on November 27, 1949, my classmates and I were confirmed. Gazing at the pastor, to me it seemed his eyes were old, his face colorless and drab. Still, I could not resist being the star. My voice boomed above my classmates as we gave the answers by rote to the confirmation lesson questions put before us. A more important lesson had already burrowed inside me: Never divulge your true feelings. By the end of that year Reverend Zoarb had been transferred and I stopped attending church.

A month to the day later, on December 27, 1949, at age fourteen, I lost my virginity on the front seat of a 1950 Buick in

Greenwood Cemetery. That deed opened the floodgates of my raging adolescent hormones, bottled up for so long. If like today, logoed T-shirts had been in vogue, I would have proudly worn one proclaiming: "So many men, so little time." But that's another story.

Ancestors of Frances Ethel Oliphant Gabino

Parents

Howard Damer Oliphant, Jr.
   b: 16 Mar., 1910 -Superior (Douglas Co.) WI. USA
   m: 16 Mar., 1933 -Concordia Lutheran Church, Superior,
WI. USA
   d: 6 June,1990 -Oakland (Douglas Co.) WI. USA

Marie Olive Larsen
   b: 1 May, 1896 -Kristiania (Garnisonsmenight) Norway
   d: 3 Aug., 1987 -Superior (Douglas Co.) WI. USA

Grandparents

Howard Damer Oliphant, Sr.
   b: 1 Sept., 1881 -Keister (Faribault Co.) MN. USA
   m: 12 Feb., 1900 -Superior (Douglas Co.) WI. USA
   d: 18 May 1956 -Grantsburg (Burnett Co.) WI. USA

Grace Darling Waterston
      b: 11 April, 1883 -Fall City (Dunn Co.) WI. USA
      d: 3 June, 1972 -Superior, (Douglas Co.) WI USA

Johan Jorgan Michael Larsen
      b: 16 May, 1866 -Vestresagene Kristiania, Norway
      m: 18 Oct., 1892 -Kristiania (Paulus Parish) Norway
      d: 10 July, 1943 -Superior (Douglas Co.) WI. USA

Laura Wilhelmina Pedersen
      b: 16 Feb., 1863 -Larvik (Jarlsberg og Larvik-
Vestfold) Norway.
      d: 9 April, 1948 -Superior (Douglas Co.) WI. USA

Great Grandparents

Frederick Oliphant
>   b: 21 Jan, 1856 -New Haven Twnsp. (Oswego, Co.) NY
>   m: 20 Oct, 1881 -Seely, MN
>   d: 1 Jan., 1888 -Wells (Faribault, Co.) MN

Annie Elizabeth Duncan
>   b: 12 Oct., 1862 -Goderich, Ontario CANADA
>   d: 23 Feb., 1957 -Superior (Douglas, Co.) WI USA

James (Jim) Waterston
>   b: 16 Feb., 1856 -Milwaukee, (Milwaukee, Co.) WI USA
>   m: 1 April, 1882 -Fall City, WI USA
>   d: 15 Jan., 1947 -Superior (Douglas, Co.) WI USA

Bessie Harshman
>   b: 11 Dec., 1861 -Fall City, WI
>   d: 4 April, 1948, Superior, WI

Gulbrand Larsen
>   b: 18 Oct., 1829 -Christiania, NORWAY
>   m: 23 Aug., 1851 -Christiania, NORWAY
>   d: 9 June, 1902 -Christiania, NORWAY

Marie Larsdatter
>   b: 21 Feb., 1829 -Langesund, NORWAY
>   d: 4 Sept., 1905 -Christiania, NORWAY

Simon Pedersen
>   b: 24 Nov., 1819 -Froen Parish, NORWAY
>   m: 30 May, 1862 -Larvik, NORWAY
>   d: 7 Feb., 1900 -Christiania, NORWAY

Anne Marie F. Petersen
>   b: 4 June, 1832 -Larvik, NORWAY
>   d: 23 March, 1896 -Larvik NORWAY

Father's Family Group Record

Husband: Howard Damer Oliphant Sr.
>Birth: 1 Sept., 1881 -Keister (Faribault Co) MN USA
>Death: 18 May, 1956 -Grantsburg, (Bennett Co) WI USA
>Marriage: 12 Feb., 1900 -Superior (Douglas Co) WI USA
>Divorce: 17 Oct., 1943 -Superior (Douglas Co) WI USA
>Father: Frederick Hosea Oliphant (b 21 Jan., 1856)
>Mother: Annie Elizabeth Duncan (b 12 Oct., 1862)

Wife: Grace Darling Waterston
>Birth: 11 April, 1883 -Fall City (Dunn Co) WI USA
>Death: 3 June, 1972 -Superior (Douglas Co) WI USA
>Father: James (Jim) Waterston (b 16 Feb., 1856)
>Mother: Bessie Harshman (b 11 Dec., 1861)

CHILDREN

1 ETHEL GRACE OLIPHANT
  Birth: 8 Jun 1900   SUPERIOR (Douglas Co) WI USA
  Death: 17 Feb 1961   SUPERIOR (Douglas Co) WI USA
  Spouse: ARTHUR GROVER WAGNER (m 13 Nov 1919)
2 MARGARET ROSE OLIPHANT (AKA: ROSE   )
  Birth: 1 Jan 1902   SUPERIOR (Douglas Co) WI USA
  Death: 10 Jun 1998 -SUPERIOR (Douglas Co) WI USA
  Spouse: THOMAS JOHN MOCKLER (m 19 Jul 1920)
3 FREDERICK JAMES OLIPHANT
  Birth: 7 Nov 1904   SUPERIOR (Douglas Co) WI USA
  Death: 16 Apr 1979   SUPERIOR (Douglas Co) WI USA
  Spouse: MYRTLE RUTH SENATE (m 10 Jun 1925)
4 HELEN MAY OLIPHANT
  Birth: 1 May 1906   SUPERIOR (Douglas Co) WI USA
  Death: 2 Dec 1996   SUPERIOR (Douglas Co) WI USA
  Spouse: PAUL WALTA (m 12 Oct 1923)
5 MILDRED RUTH OLIPHANT
  Birth: 2 May 1908   SUPERIOR (Douglas Co) WI USA
    Spouse: RUDOLPH FRED "RUDY" LARSON (m 25 Jul 1924)
6 HOWARD DAMER JR. OLIPHANT
  Birth: 16 Mar 1910   SUPERIOR (Douglas Co) WI USA
  Death: 6 Jun 1990   SUPERIOR (Douglas Co) WI USA
  Spouse: MARIE OLIVE LARSEN (m 16 Mar 1933)
7 ROBERT DUNCAN OLIPHANT
  Birth: 25 Sep 1913   SUPERIOR (Douglas Co) WI USA
  Death: 8 Jun 1995   OLYMPIA (Thurston Co) WA USA
  Spouse: MARIANNE SCAAF ZAHN (m 20 Feb 1952)

Mother's Family Group Record

Husband: JOHAN JORGAN MICHAEL LARSEN
Birth: 16 May, 1866 -KRISTIANIA, (Vestre Sagene) NORWAY
Baptism: 26 Aug 1866 -KRISTIANIA (Paulus) NORWAY.
Census: 1900 -SKILLINGS GADE #8 LARVIK
Immigration: 22 Sep., 1903 -Larvik (Larvik-Vestfold) NORWAY
Emigration: 3 Oct., 1903 -SUPERIOR (Douglas Co) WI USA
Death: 10 Jul., 1943 -SUPERIOR (Douglas Co) WI USA
Burial: 14 Jul 1943 Riverside Cem., Superior (Douglas Co) WI
Nationality: NORWEGIAN
Marriage: 18 Oct., 1892 KRISTIANIA (Paulus) NORWAY
Father: GULBRAND LARSEN (b 18 Oct 1829)
Mother: MARIE OLAVA LARSDATTER (b 21 Feb 1829)
Wife: LAURA WILHELMINA PEDERSEN
Birth: 16 Feb 1863   LARVIK (Vestfold) NORWAY
Baptism: 28 Apr 1864   LARVIK (Larvik - Vestfold) NORWAY
Death: 9 Apr 1948 SUPERIOR (Douglas Co) WI USA
Burial: 13 Apr 1948 Riverside Cem. Superior (Douglas Co) WI
Nationality: NORWEGIAN
Father: SIMON PEDERSEN (b 24 Nov 1819)
Mother: ANNE MARIE F PETERSEN (b 4 Jun 1832)

Children

1 GUNNAR STEFAN LARSEN
   Birth: 16 Jun., 1893 -KRISTIANIA (Paulus) NORWAY
   Death: 14 Mar., 1967 -DETROIT (Wayne Co) MI USA
   Marriage: To Frances Niece (date unknown)

2. MARIE OLIVE LARSEN
 Birth: 1 May 1896 -KRISTIANIA (Paulus) NORWAY
 Baptism: 31 May, 1896 -Paulus Menighed, Kristiania Norway
 Death: 3 Aug., 1987 -SUPERIOR (Douglas Co) WI USA
 Burial: 6 Aug. 1987 Riverside Cem. Superior (Douglas Co)WI
 Spouse: HOWARD DAMER JR OLIPHANT (m 16 Mar 1933)

Author Bio

Born and raised in Superior, Wisconsin Frances graduated from Wm. C. Bryant Grade School in 1949, from Central High School, in 1953. Her first job was at Western Electric, Duluth MN; as a solderer. In 1955 she lived in Chicago for a short time, returned to Superior and worked at Crystal Waters Lodge, Grand Rapids, MN. Back in Chicago in 1956, she began her thirty-four year tenure at American National Bank & Trust Company, 33 N. LaSalle St.; as a company cafeteria employee, rising from various clerical positions, to Security Vault Manager. During her years at American National, Frances attended classes at the YMCA, Chicago City Junior College and Northeastern IL. Univ. where at the latter institution, in 1989, she received her BA degree in Communications/Creative Writing.

During her Chicago years Frances traveled extensively in Greece, Great Britain, the Netherlands and Norway, as well as the United States. She was married to Ernesto Garcia Gabino from 1959 to 1972.

In 1990 Frances took early retirement and returned to Superior, to part-time work for Manpower Inc., Duluth, MN; Garon Knitting and K-Mart, Superior, followed by five years as a home-care provider.

Since returning to Superior, Frances has attended writing workshops at The Depot, Duluth, MN; Univ. of Iowa, Iowa City IA; and at Fergus Falls Community College, Fergus Falls, MN. Besides creative writing, her interests include genealogy, history, and Norwegian culture. She is a thirty-three year member of Sons of Norway, and numerous genealogical societies.

"It is a good rule in life never to apologize. The right sort of people do not want apologies, and the wrong sort take a mean advantage of them."

— P.G. Wodehouse

Other Savage Press Books Available

Poetry

In the Heart of the Forest by Diana Randolph
Appalachian Mettle by Paul Bennett
Treasures from the Beginning of the World by Jeff Lewis
Gleanings from the Hillsides, Philosophical Poems,
Poems of Faith and Inspiration, three books by E.M. Johnson
Thicker Than Water by Hazel Sangster
Mystic Bread by Mike Savage
Moments Beautiful Moments Bright by Brett Bartholomaus
Pathways by Mary B. Wadzinski, *Treasured Thoughts* by Sierra

Fiction

The Year of the Buffalo, a novel of love and minor league baseball
by Marshall J. Cook
Something in the Water, Burn Baby Burn by Mike Savage
Voices from the North Edge by St. Croix Writers
Keeper of the Town by Don Cameron
The Lost Locomotive of the Battle-Axe by Mike Savage

Nonfiction

Business

SoundBites by Kathy Kerchner
Dare to Kiss the Frog by van Hauen, Kastberg & Soden

Sports and Travel

Sailboat Log Book by Don Handy, Illus. by Gordon Slotness
Canoe & Kayaker's Floating Log Book by Don Handy
The Duluth Tour Book & the North Shore Tour Book
by Jeff Cornelius

Essay, Humor, Reminiscence

Hometown Wisconsin by Marshall J. Cook
Jackpine Savages by Frank Larson
The Awakening of the Heart by Jill Downs
Widow of the Waves by Bev Jamison

Local & Regional History

Stop in the Name of the Law by Alex O'Kash
Beyond the Mine by Peter J. Benzoni
Some Things You Never Forget by Clem Miller
Superior Catholics by Cheney and Meronek

To order additional copies of

Crocodile Tears
and
Lipstick Smears

or receive a copy of the complete
Savage Press catalog,

contact us at:

Phone Orders: 1-800-732-3867

Voice and Fax: (715) 394-9513

e-mail: savpress@spacestar.com

Visit online at: www.savpress.com

Visa or MasterCard accepted

Box 115, Superior, WI 54880 (715) 394-9513